REALITY *of* *Reality*

BOOK ONE

BRETT PEARCE

A Disciple and Servant of the Most High God
called in a dream

By the grace of God this book is presented to..

NAME:______________________________

PLACE: ______________________________

DATE:______________________________

BY:______________________________

ISBN 978-1-73955-990-8 (softcover)

Word of Life Books
author@wordoflifebooks.info

Reality of Reality Movements 1-21

Reality of Reality
Movements 22-42

Cross-reference

ABOUT THIS BOOK

Written firstly: To the honor and glory of the most high God, composed out of real life and dath struggles of the flesh and spirit, brought out of faith in God's word, enhanced by the camera like effects to recall and remember the resemblance effects that are uncovered by the power of the holy spirit, not restricted by time or space, power or opposition in all aspects in every situation or facet of ones life for good and right.

And that the true loving nature of God exists in His willingness to deliver and save all flesh, manifest in the sending of His only begotten son Jesus Christ, whom is both true man and true God to pay for the sins of man [with his life on the cross] for there is no greater love.

Parallel to the activities of the Lord in heaven and on earth throughout history of mankind is the Original King James Bible **OKJB**, not

pg 175 to be interfered with.. **Revelation 22:v18-19.**

Read *For I testify unto every man that hears the words of the prophecy of the book, if any man shall add unto these things, God shall add unto him the plagues that are written in this book.*

*And if any man shall take away from the words of this prophecy, God shall take away his part out of the Holy city, and from the things which are written in this book.. [**Revelation 22:v18-19**]..*

Written secondly: To fulfill His will upon His servant, that His house on earth may be filled, .. **Luke 14:v23** to go to, to reach out to all nations and compel them to come in, to those whom are near and far. to the poor, the rich, leaders, royalty

Cross-reference

pp 5 / 18

princes, princesses, governors, teachers, parents and individuals, to six of the seven churches recorded in **Revelation** chapters **2** and **3** of the **OKJB,** anyone and all everywhere located and sort out from among the high ways and hedges.

Read **Luke chapter 14.**.read from your **OKJB.** You have now been called **v23** choose to accept this call and come to the one Holy Altar of the Lord where the apostle ministry is actively preparing the bride for the marriage supper. **Written thirdly:** To expose and pin point any works of the evil one, commonly known as the devil and how to recognize that he has you in his grip, and what you need to do for Jesus to release you from this grip that can lead to eternal death and torment, there is no other way and starts with two choices, Jesus and yours.

RR And so this book has **42** ***Reality of Reality*** movements, these movements come too or about through fixtures by way of everyday actions by the choices that we make and how, hence my saying

RR ***(Reality of Reality)*** and title of my books.

These books will reveal untruths, lies, deceptions, manipulations, partialities and folly, the truth through non matching or matching.

WHAT TO EXPECT FROM THIS BOOK :
Reveal and explain mysteries, miracles, places and positions., these are for to the Kingdom of God on earth, a glimpse into the real workings of the living word of God, they tell how to be convinced God is busy at work in your life, or cant be and if God cant, means the devil is and you are not in his kingdom, this is the reality of reality the title of this book. To make it easy through a comprehensive set of teachings how to measure these workings on the scale of balances that are to be found within the Old and New testaments of the **OKJB**.

Cross-reference

RR therefore it is justly right to say that in addition to the the right Holy Bible this book ***Reality of Reality*** has been composed out of real life living the original Gospel of Christ word of life, to fulfill the words of Jesus Christ. **John 14: v12** Verily, verily I say unto you, He that believes on me, the works that I do, he do also; and greater works than these shall he do; because I go unto my Father.. **[John 14:v12..**

WHAT YOU WILL GET IN THIS BOOK

RR The truth!! spoken with love, teachings that are hard to come by in church services unveiled through ***Reality of Reality*** movements, the veil of the temple was torn in two, from top to the bottom.. **Mark15:v37-38**..words alone will not cause the right movement, if there is no two part movement at all, there has to be words and action, then comes the understanding, which is the movement.

Read *And Jesus cried with a loud voice, and gave up the Ghost. And the veil of the temple was rent in twain from the top to the bottom..*
..[Mark 15:v37-38]..

WHAT YOU WILL GET FROM THIS BOOK

Your life will change, you will do things differently you will see things clearer and things you have not seen before, no person will be able to mislead you filled with the courage of faith, the fear of not knowing will be no more, sleeping will be with rest true peace will be a new condition, this world will become less interesting, sometimes you will find yourself looking down at it, true freedom and salvation is now reachable and touchable, rebirth will be happening.. **John 3:v3..**

pg 8

Read *Jesus answered and said unto him, verily verily I say unto thee, Except a man be born again, he cannot see the kingdom of God.*
..[John 3:v3]..

Cross-reference

WHAT YOU NEED TO DO WITH THIS BOOK

RR Work through the ***Reality of Reality*** movements as they come your way or as they appear in your life, not the other way round, don't try to make them happen, use the teachings and explanations given, get yourself the original king James bible, dated 1611, read and

RR pray on your knees specific to the ***reality of reality*** movement.

REALITY OF REALITY MOVEMENTS: I was at school today its true **[reality 1]** yet I learned nothing its true **[reality 2]** no movement. OR I was at school today its true **[reality 1]** I learned how to calculate its true **[reality 2]** movement. OR I am a leader it's the truth **[reality 1]** yet I lead my people into poverty it's the truth **[reality 2]** no right movement. OR I am a Christian it's the truth **[reality 1]** and I obey the new commandments it's the truth **[reality 2]** right movement. what is sown is reaped.. **Galatians 6:v7**..

Read *Be not deceived; God is not mocked: for whatsoever a man sows, that shall he also*

pg 28 *reap.. **[Galatians 6:v7]***

HOW AND WHEN TO USE THIS BOOK Keep this book with you wherever you go its small enough, and has some bible references for this purpose, it has been compiled for everyday everywhere use. Take it out: On the bus, the train, during break, sitting in your car parked, in bed. Everything comes by way of practice and repetition, it may be happen that it takes two

Cross-reference

experiences before your eyes see the full message out your encounter with Jesus Christ.. **Mark 8:v22-25**..that second time can come years later too.

Read ..*[**Mark 8:v22-25**].. And he (Jesus) cometh to Beth-sa'i-da: and they bring a blind man unto him, and besought him to touch him. And he took the blind man by the hand, and led him out of the town; and when he had spit on his eyes, and put his hands upon him, he asked him if he saw ought. And he looked up, and said, I see men as trees, walking. After that he put his hands again upon his eyes, and made him look up: and he was restored, and saw every man clearly,*

pg 164

Read *See that none render evil for evil unto any man;but ever follow that which is good both among yourselves, and to all men. Rejoice evermore. Pray without ceasing [**1 Thessalonians** ***5:v15-17***]..*

pg 141

THE COVER:

And the Lord said unto the servant, Go out into the high ways and hedges, and compel them to come in, that My house may be filled..[**Luke 14:v23**].

Sketches: a mountain and blue sky, clouds, **a** boat **setting sail** (**a winding** road going up hill with hedges on either side).

pp 2/ 18

Man and Woman, Sky and Air, Water, and dwellings, colors.. white, yellow, blue, a cross in the sky.

Husband and wife together spreading

RR the GOOD NEWS ***Reality ofReality*** .

Cross-reference

CONTACT PAGE:

Brett G Pearce.. Author
Mobile +44 7830 803663
Home phone : +44 7830 803663

Website : wordoflifebooks.info
E-Mail : author@wordoflifebooks.info
By letter: 80 Lant avenue, Llandrindod Wells Powys LD15EH Wales UK.

REQUESTS:

Ask questions.
Appearances.
Counseling.
Interviews.
Prayer.
Other.

FACTS AND FIGURES

- 60, OOO words
- 370+ Bible verses
- 370 + Cross references
- 50 + years of my life covered
- 30 + years in ministry

ABBREVIATIONS

- ***OKJVB*** *= original king James bible*
- ***RR*** *= Reality of Reality*
- ***PG*** *= page*
- ***PP*** *= pages*
- ***NAC*** *= New apostolic church*
- ***CR*** *= Cross page reference*

Cross-reference

ABOUT ME THE AUTHOR

I Brett George Pearce later called in a dream by the Almighty God to be His servant yet learn that Christ really existed by [a simple prayer] years before bringing to life this bible verse, **Isaiah 46 : v10** : Declaring the end from the beginning that would set the trend for my future lifestyle and learning, the essence of this book and how I teach, knowing the Gospel word after first living it, yet not realizing back then what was happening to me, a mystery that was to unfold years later in miraculous ways.

Read *Declaring the end from the beginning, and from ancient times the things that are not yet done. My counsel shall stand, and I will do all My pleasure..**[Isaiah 46:v10]**..*

Back to the simple prayer

A PRAYER OUT OF MY HEART...

Please Jesus don't let my MUM die, I was just 13 years old .. Two separate incidents or attempts where my mother attempted to end her life committing suicide by overdosing with her tablets, it was during these two suicide attempts, that I went into the nearby Rochester Cathedral (for a Godly reason for a change I might add) sat in the pew looked up to heave and uttered those seven words in total belief, culminating in an array of mixed emotions and feelings.

My prayers were answered, my mum did not die but live, both times, this stuck with me in my sub conscious though, only to re-surface 15 years later after I had spent a fair amount of the broad way, and after I had met up with my ex-wife and joined the new apostolic church **NAC.** (still connected with), more on this church in

Book 2 RR ***Reality of Reality*** book 2, after

Cross-reference

seeing and hearing things that were of peculiar interest to me, I had recognize that there was something great and separate, life changing in where I had now found myself, that would begin to cause me to sell everything that I had spiritually accumulated in the field of life, to purchase this heavenly treasure.

Read

Again, the kingdom of heaven is like unto treasure hid in a field; the which when a man hath found ,he hides, and for joy here of goes and sells all that he has and buys that field.. [Matthew 13:v44]

pp 248 /290

In this position of words and Holy Acts, mysteriously and timely matching my then current thinking, it was **NEW** ,I was to get involved, before even knowing what this **NAC** believed, or what it teachings was about yet I began to see my new life unfolding yet could not be seen with the natural eye, the spiritual, through re birth.

A fine thread of simple truth words with a life style to match [a narrow way, strait gait] filled with revealed mysteries and wonders began to emerge and I willingly accepted the call, was adopted into this house hold of God, got water and spirit baptized, three steps to my new life had begun, the rebirth.. **John 3:v5.**

pg 3

Read

*Jesus answered, Verily, verily I say unto thee, Except a man be born of water and spirit he can not enter the kingdom of God. [**John 3:v5**]*

Quickly and swiftly I soon began to gain Godly knowledge and wisdom, through dedicated prayer and perseverance, to do right after having done so much wrong, living a life in the broad way [world]

Cross-reference

that had to be undone and replaced, this is the spiritual rebirth, then narrow way and it would be this way that would be the grindstone in the tool sharpening process, honing in a kind of readiness to be a sharp two edged sword in the Lord's hand, the essence of this book for which I owe all to God. It was during my 28th year, less than a year into my new found path, that the dream happened, it is by the authenticity of this dream that has enabled me to remain that sharpened two edge sword in the hand of God to this day, amidst the many opposing forces giving rise to many sorrows in my life, the evil one had inflicted yet through all those temptations, come in by way of those closest and dearest to me the nearby yet I managed to remain firmly embedded on the only rock of salvation **Psalm 62:v6/7**..

Read ***..[Psalm 62:v6-7]..*** *He only is my rock and my salvation; He is my defense, I shall not be moved, in God is my salvation and glory; the rock of my strength, and my refuge is in God.*

The Lord continues with me leading me where He wants me to be and sending me where He wants me to go, both in the spirit and the physical places, moving me on from time to time as per His will to achieve His purpose. Not a just only renewed spiritual life has been unveiled and beset in me, a brand new natural life too, for God who is able to keep all His covenants and promises has restored my fortunes as he had done with Job who stuck it out with him, allowing himself not to be influenced by family and friends whom

Cross-reference

learned harsh lessons from his faithful servant, which stand today as a living testimony of the only one to be trusted and relied on is the most high God.. **Job 42:9-17..Mark 10 :v29**

Read

And the Lord turned the captivity of Job, when he prayed for his friends: also the Lord gave twice as much as he had before.. ***[Job 42:v10].*** *and also* ***[Mark 10:v29]*** *. And Jesus answered and said; Verily I say unto you, There is no man that hath left house, or brethren, or sisters, or father, or mother, or wife, or children, or lands, for my sake and the gospel* ***[v30]****..But he shall receive an hundredfold now in this time.*

MY: CREDENTIALS AS A SERVANT OF GOD..

I was called by God through a dream.

After having received the ministry of sub deacon by the laying on of hands of the living apostle of Jesus as seen in my dream, I set about working in the work of God first in His church second in my personal vineyard, actually even before the dream and sub deacon ministry I was active in both, at this time I was being mentored by a senior priest, he would tell me do not aspire after a ministry, serving the Lord is not based only on ministry, little did he or I know, God was using him. I received two other ministries through the laying on of hands of a living apostle as is the order of God in both testament times.. **Numbers 27:v18.. Acts 6:v6**..

Read

And the Lord said unto Moses, Take thee Joshua the son of Nun, a man in whom is the spirit, and lay thine hand upon him. ***Numbers.. [27:v18] [Acts 6:v6]****..Whom they set before the apostles,*

Cross-reference

Read *and when they had prayed, they laid their hands on them.*

The deacon ministry then came the ministry of priest, by this time my newly found occupation had become my number one, my first love.. **Revelation2:v4** ..The New apostolic church, I continued to grow in my ministerial activities along with spiritual knowledge, however this brought in separation between my ex-wife and me, and a divide with the apostle men [not ministry] ultimately we stood no more as one flesh but divded..**Mark3:v25**.

I would experience what it really IS to have a broken heart [twice] God broke in my soul and spirit (His word was rejected) by my wife and the apostles whom took her side ..**Psalm147:v3**.. Yet He soon healed me through His word brought by the holy spirit in grace.

Read *Nevertheless, I have some what against thee, because thou has left thy first love..* ***[Revelation..2:v4... [Mark3:v25]***.

And if a house be divided against itself, that house cannot stand. He heals the broken in heart ,and binds up their wounds. ***[Psalm 147:v3]***..

By the time complete and full separation had come through divorce, I had been thrown into jail, lost my business of 25 years, my home got sold, my two children had dispersed, was wrongfully removed from serving as priest in the New apostolic church, I believed to be the real church of Jesus church, meaning: both in the physical and spiritual, for surely some members at the time put their entire life into it as I also did, this however does not take away or reduce the holiness brought through the presence of God in the holy spirit today. God knows the truth and still uses me today,

Cross-reference

this is His evidence and I will be His witness reserved for the day of judgment to come upon my adversaries in the event it goes all that way.. **John 8:v9**.. and.. **1 Peter 4:v17**..

Read

*And they which heard it, being convicted by their own conscience, went out one by on, beginning at the eldest, even unto the last: and Jesus was left alone, and the woman standing in the midst..**[John 8:v9]**.. **[1 Peter 4:v17]**.. For the time is come that judgment must begin at the house of God, and if it first begin at us, what shall the end be of them that obey not in the gospel of God..*

Book 2

RR

MORE TO COME: On the ***New Apostolic Church***, and why you should accept the call to come and see for yourself the Holy Acts and gifts of salvation to be found and had here after receiving the invitation through the ***Reality of Reality movements*** teaching, certainly there is a congregation accessible to you and your whole family.

RR

Also more on my serving as the holy spirit leads me, my restored good fortunes and a renewed family life, bible verses lived, experiences of faith, mysteries and wonders revealed, new dreams, my convictions and battles, more about these two: the Original Church Activities and the Original King James Bible, these and more will be added into the ***Reality of Reality*** books to come. Of course all by the good righteous will of and grace of my Abba Father.

Cross-reference

ACKNOWLEDGEMENTS

TO: THE ALMIGHTY LORD GOD

First: has to be to the Almighty Lord God for His willingness to go all out to save souls that He has created out of love..

John 3:v16.. in revealing Himself through His only begotten son JesusChrist.

For His unfathomable love, patience and long suffering not willing that anyone should be lost.

For creating and providing all the means to servants, the real church, Holy Acts and sacraments, the technologies:

Alphabets, Paper, Printing, Ink,Computer, radio waves etc.

Read *For God so loved the world, that He gave His only begotten son, that whosoever believes in him should not perish, but have everlasting life.* ***[John 3:v16]***

pp 194 /276/210

TO: JESUSUS CHRIST OUR LORD

For the ultimate sacrifice of love, the crucifixion on the cross.. **Mark 15:v24 and v25**..

Read *And when they had crucified him, they parted his garments, casting lots upon them, what every man should take..* ***[Mark15:v24]***

[Mark 15:v25].. *And it was the third hour, and they crucified him.*

Read *I,even I, am he that blots out thy transgressions, for mine own sake, and will not remember thy sins.* ***[Isaiah 43:v25]..***

TO: KING JAMES AND THE SOME 47 PLUS BIBLICAL SCHOLARS AND TRANSLATORS FOR THE OKJB.

Certainly for me and everyone everywhere this masterful contribution is good enough to learn of and come close too the one true God and His will for the future new kingdoms.

Cross-reference

TO: THE TRUE GIFTS..
REAL FAITHFUL DISCIPLES, FROM THE ORIGINAL CHURCH OF JESUS CHRIST AND THE NAC.
THE APOSTLE MINISTRY.
THE HOLY SPIRIT/GHOST.

Men and women of faith standing firmly on the one true Gospel of Christ in suffering, accepting and not receiving any earthly gain but loss, your teaching through example remains with me.
District Elder Dieter Korner, Priest Ted Henry Priest Sydney Saunders, Shepherd Theo Hendricks.. Sister Glodina Snyman, Sister Ina Van Dyk.. to name some.
The activity of the Apostle ministry that allows Jesus real church to be exist and set apart from all others.
The Holy Spirit that really has comforted me through the transformation of re-birth.

To my previous wife **Colleen** of 25 years I am thankful to you for allowing God to use you in bringing me into the church of Christ.

MY DEAR WIFE
Mrs Belina Pearce I am in-love with you my sweetheart, first faithful to God, neighbors and then me, supporting me in all areas of my life that is right, challenging me in areas not, supporting me especially in my ministry so that I will fulfill the call and gift given to me by God in a dream helping me through all my challenges.
We are truly by the power and grace of God one flesh.. **Mark 10:v7/8**

Read *For this cause shall a man leave his father and mother, and cleave to his wife And they twain shall be one flesh: so then they are no more twain, but one flesh..* ***[Mark 7-8]***

Cross-reference

YOU MY NEIGHBOUR

To ALL and anyone that God has used along my way, to those who gave me employment, were patient with me whilst learning new tasks and to those who supported me in some way or other, to all those who put up with my harping on these biblical subjects, to all those who were not at all sincere, and those who were just sincere, all things work together.. **Romans 8:v28**..

Read *And we know that all things work together for good to them that love God, to them who are called according to his purpose.. **[Romans 8:v28]***

Fernande's Siazilombo [elder in the NAC]

Thank you for all your support from afar, when the holy Ghost prompted you always answered and obeyed very willingly knowing it was for the Lord, you surely will be and are a witness to the love of God on earth and in heaven.

Betty Weal now deceased Whom supported us financially and truthfully when I was out of work and had no income.. May God bless your coming in and going out for accepting the call too.

Sally Anne Pearce my dear sister For her support financially to make this book become
RR a ***Reality of Reality*** and happen.

John Farrow, My true friend, helper and confidant.

THE PUBLISHERS

Brett and Belina Pearce for word of life books.

Cross-reference

THE WEBSITE DEVELOPER

Gary Simons of SA.

Contact details are :
Gary Simons
Gary@sitesculptor.co.za
Phone : +27 824085119

To those who are not mentioned, It is with the Almighty God

Cross-reference

THE FIRST REALITY

INTRODUCTION

It is real, there are those persons going back to the beginning of mankind that have tasted the grace and mercy of God through Jesus Christ and his real servants, yet have either fallen away or show themselves to be true to the way but are not, God alone knows who they are really.. **Matthew 22:v12/13**..

Read

..[**Matthew** *22:v12-13]*.. *And He says unto him friend, how came you on here not having a wedding garment? And he was speechless.*
*..**[v13]..**Then said the God the King to the servants, Bind him hand and foot, and take him away, and cast him into outer darkness; there shall be gnashing of teeth, such are those whom will find themselves amongst the Gnashes of teeth, those separated from the true followers of Christ, His servants presently active in the earthly and spiritual realms in finding and preparing a bride for the King's son Jesus to be ready at his return, also referred to in Holy Scripture as virgin**s.***
..Mathew 25:v1-13]..

Read

..[**Matthew 25:v1-13]..** Below are verses that pertained to the five foolish virgins..[**v8**].. And the foolish said unto the wise,Give us of your oil for our lamps are gone out .. [**v11]..** Afterward also came these virgins saying, Lord, lord open for us..[**v12]**.. But he answered and said, Verily verily I say unto you I know you not.

pg 73

Cross-reference

There are those that the lord called, yet did not take their call to be part of the Marriage to Jesus Christ sure and so will not be elected to be part of the bride of Christ (groom) which will take place in heaven, after his return..**2 Peter 1:v10**..

Read *Wherefore the rather, brethren, give diligence to make your calling and election sure; for if you do these things ye shall never fail.. **[2 peter 1:v10]**..*

THE SECOND REALITY

It is real that there are predestined souls out there in the highways and hedges the Lord has predestined to call to come to marriage supper in heaven destined soon to take place.. **Luke 14:v23**..

Read *And the Lord said unto the servant, Go out into the highways and hedges, and compel them to come in, that My house may be filled.. **[Luke 14:v23]***

There is about to be a marriage and a feast in the heavenly realm, the groom is the King's son Jesus Christ, the King is God; He is mentioned in..5.18.. This not a secret, many have been called and know what is expected of them, these are to make up the bride for the groom, they are simple everyday people coming out of the worlds nations, yet made virgin pure by participating in the life and death of Jesus, actually his blood, that is the wedding garment. This book is to reach out: invite or call, just as I was, even to the far out places, no one is to be excluded from the invitation, highways symbolizes; up and out from the cities into the

Cross-reference

hills and valleys, hedges symbolizes; the hidden places which the Lord knows, He will direct His servant, lead his servant, send him. There is enough room for more to come because some that are called had not made themselves ready, hence the the right garment required they did not put on, and because the date had been set, it had to happen, there could not be a delay. This book is to make hearing the call easy, yet for those who acknowledge the call will need to make the call sure, some effort and work will be required, yet with God all things are possible.

Read *But Jesus beheld them, and said unto them, with men this is impossible, but with God all things are possible..[**Matthew 19:v26**]..*

ALL VERSES ARE TAKEN OUT FROM THE ORIGINAL KING JAMES BIBLE 1611

NOTES

Reality *of* ***Reality***

MOVEMENT NUMBER 1

Sleeping

Without a life in Christ, there can be no proper rest or peace in this life or the next, going to sleep without sleeping

Cross-reference

SLEEPING

Lots can happen to us as we sleep, it can be a pleasant and beneficial experience or quite the opposite, too much sleep is detrimental to a successful goal focused life and also leaves a person vulnerable.. **Mark 14:v37-38**.. Sleep is linked to death, also referred as rest certainly the closest one can be to being dead, yet just sleeping, this is how close death is to sleep, sleep is linked to no contact with Jesus Christ for Jesus is life.. **Matthew 9:v24**..

Read *And he cometh and finds them sleeping, and says unto Peter, sleepest thou? Couldest not thou watch one hour? Watch Ye and pray, lest ye enter into temptation, the spirit truly is ready, but the flesh is weak..**[Mark 14:v37-38]**..*

Read ***.[Matthew9:v24]*** *..He said unto them, Give place:for the maid is not dead, but sleeps, and they laughed him to scorn.*

The physical body after having been on the go for several or more hours needs to rest and re new itself, therefore sleep is a gift, one of those unrecognizable gifts from God, night time then is the second component of this gift, when all people are to bed down at the same time, this stillness has exceptional healing qualities, when recognized and embraced. Of course as with anything, preparation and timing is key, to bed down for a good night sleep one must be in the right state, both body and mind must be at peace with each other, there has to be harmony, if the body had been up to wrong doings or over indulged in things of the world, its likely that

Cross-reference

the opportunity to relax properly as should be happening doesn't and one goes off to sleep yet

RR not able too, the ***reality of reality*** is not matching, one is lying down in their bed the first reality yet cannot rest the second reality something is wrong, scripture that is the Holy Bible says it should not be that way.. **Proverbs 3:v24**..

Read *When thou lay down, thou shalt not be afraid: Yea shalt lie down and thy sleep shall be sweet..* ***[Proverbs 3v24]***..

When in the sleep state, the physical body allows the spirit of that person to make itself known, how it is, whats really going on inside a kind of pre-death inspection that one should take very seriously, most common are dreams which tell what is really going on inside, often not making any natural sense, yet give clues that something to be done, change is required, the truth of this matter is this: if? Unity between body, soul and spirit are not there in the good sense or state and one can accept this condition is not right, something must be done to change this situation or state, again turning to the one who can help, the one who knows everything, Jesus Christ whom himself needed to sleep and rest... **Matthew 8:v24**..Often what keeps people from a good sleep is there life style striving for earthly status and wealth or simply just being anxious about the trials of life and come under

pg 203 burdens.. **Matthew 11:v28**..

Read *And behold there arose a great tempest in the sea insomuch that the ship was covered with the waves, but he was asleep..* ***[Matthew 8:v24]***

Cross-reference

Read *[**Matthew 11:v28**].. Come unto me, all ye that labor and are heavy laden, and I will give you rest.*

RR ***reality of reality*** is to go to sleep but not rest.

One is naturally vulnerable when asleep; spiritually also, all humans have the same enemy and he is out to destroy our eternal rest. The devil or wicked one, does this through temptations, when one has entered into temptation during times of being physically active, which can happen during the day or night time these works of evil will accumulate and rob people of their much needed rest and peace, these two qualities are the absence of all toiling, on when reaching this perfect state, one is in perfect harmony with their body soul and spirit, then just the thought of going to bed at night.. is sweet.

The right example to use about perfect rest after laboring or working, is God, He said, I quote after I had created the world and all it contains, I rested from all my labors, declaring that His works were good.. **Genesis 1:v31** and **Genesis 2:v2** there are also bad works, God doesn't and cannot do bad works or harm anyone yet people can when they follow the wicked one through temptation to do evil.. **Matthew 26:v41**..

Read *[**Genesis 1:v31**].. And God saw everything that He had made, and, behold, it was very good, and the evening and the morning were the sixth day.. [**Genesis 2:v2**].. And on the seventh day, God ended His work which He had made; and He rested ion the seventh day from all His work which He had made.*

Cross-reference

Back to preparing for a good peaceful sleep, this takes place during the time one is awake and what they are busy with, how they conduct their daily lives, what things are of interest and occupy their lives will play the same role in the time of sleep, if one is selfish or greedy looking out only for themselves, their own rich interests and not for others, it will be difficult to switch over to a perfect sleep, similarly a life that denies the existence of a living loving God will not likely be able to recognize His presence during sleep,

RR the ..***Reality of Reality*** again is this; though its time to sleep the night has come and the bed is all fresh and made ready, the expected peaceful rest doesn't..

pp 26 /245 /278 / 169

Read **Luke 16: 19-25..**

There was a certain rich man, which was clothed in purple and fine linen, and fared sumptuously every day: and there was a certain beggar named Lazarus, which was laid at his gate, full of sores. And desiring to be fed with the crumbs which fell from the rich mans table: moreover the dogs came and licked his sores, And it came to pass that the beggar died, and was carried by the angels into Abraham's bosom, the rich man also died and was buried; and in hell he lifted up his eyes being in torments and sees Abraham afar off, and Lazarus in his bosom. And he cried and said, Father Abraham, hath mercy on me, and send Lazarus that he may dip his finger in water, and cool my tongue; for I am tormented in this flame But Abraham said, son remember that thou in thy lifetime received thy good

Cross-reference

Read

things: but now he is comforted and thou art tormented.. ***[Luke 16:19-25]***..

pp 25 /245 /278 /169

READ : **FROM VERSE 26-31.**

REALITY *of* ***REALITY***

MOVEMENT NUMBER 2

Everything Works the Same

Saying one thing and doing another has the same result now and forever.

Cross-reference

EVERYTHING WORKS THE SAME This is nature in its most simplest form, everything works the same, I learned this through life, living in the fast lane, trying to keep up with others, trying to have more, be better, living life without God actually produces nothing, this nothing means goodness, sowing to the flesh.. **Galatians 6: v7-9**..

Be not deceived; God is not mocked: for whatsoever a man sows, that shall he also reap. For he that sows to his flesh, shall of the flesh reap corruption, but he that sows to the spirit, shall of the spirit reap everlasting. And let us not be weary in well doing: for in due season, we shall reap, if we faint not.. **[Galatians 6:v7-9]..**

pg 4

An apple seed brings forth an apple tree that brings forth apples, it is not any other way, no other fruit, that mountain is over there, it is not in another place it is where it is, it stands in its position, the same with that forest or tree, they, it, are planted where they are planted, standing right where they are, yet no matter which direction a tree falls, it will lie where it fell. **Ecclesiastes 11: v3**. God the Almighty creator of heaven and earth makes understanding Him so easy how everything works the same so simple, who God Himself is, He is who He is in fact, God said unto Moses, **"I AM THAT I AM"**..**Exodus 3:v14**..

Read *If the clouds be full of rain, they empty themselves upon the earth: and if the tree falls to the south, or toward the north, in the place where the tree there it shall be..**[Ecclesiastes 11:v3]** ..*

Read [***Exodus 3:v14***].. *And God said unto Moses.. I*

Cross-reference

Read *am that I am and he said, thus shalt thou say unto the children of Israel, I am hath sent me unto you.*

Everything is recorded in heaven and on earth, mankind will get away with zero a lie will remain a lie and a commandment of God broken "the two" always the two, bearing false witness. **Exodus 20:v15/16**..stealing; taking something that is not owned, all is seen and known to the creator whom sees everything.. **Proverbs 15:v3**.. And if there is no repentant action, the same will remain until judgment day..

Read *..[**Exodus 20:v15/16**]..Thou shalt not steal, bear false witness against thy neighbor. The eyes of the Lord are in every place, beholding the evil and the good..[**Proverbs 15:v3**].. For whosoever shall keep the whole law, and yet offend in one point, he is guilty of all..[**James 2:v10**]..*

pg 239

pg 163

Portraying to be a devout follower of Jesus yet consistently even secretly breaking any of the ten commandments; knowingly and wittingly will remain that ***Reality of Reality*** if it goes all the way to judgment. THE SAME Everything works the same so says **James 2:v10..**the servant of Jesus Christ, this is God the creator, Him in his nature and character, nothing and no one can change this. To teach others to wrong knowingly, that person will be called the least in the kingdom of heaven.. likewise to teach others right the same shall be called great in the kingdom of heaven.

RR

pp 130 /143 /214 /100

Read *Whosoever shall break one of these least commandments, and shall teach men so, he shall be called the least in the kingdom of heaven: but whosoever shall do and teach them,*

Cross-reference

Read *the same shall be called great in the kingdom of heaven..**[Matthew 5: v19]**.. A good example that everything works the same*

One for Christians! It will have very serious consequences,maybe to the point of no return by continuing to ignore wrong doings,more so for those whom God has predestined and given correction (Grace) Christians after having reached the point of rebirth that return to old Adam traits could be in for a different end to their life than what they thought, scripture holds nothing back.. **1 Corinthians 11:v27**..

Read *Wherefore: whosoever so shall eat this bread, and drink this cup of the Lord, unworthily, shall be guilty of the body blood of the Lord..**[1 Corinthians 11:v27]***

Everything works the same, the outcome will be determined by choice, God has given mankind the freedom to choose one out of two options, either for Him or against Him, to be for Him, one must freely choose to bow down to Jesus Christ.. **Philippians 2:v10-11..**To obey and worship him in following his written and physical examples as is recorded in the original king James Bible, will be to free. Choosing not to bow to Jesus Christ means the same in that all that Jesus Christ is, will work against that person or persons, to condemn and not free.

Read *That at the name of Jesus every knee shall bow, of things in heaven, and things in the earth, and things under the earth. And that every tongue shall confess that Jesus Christ is Lord, to the glory of God the Father.. **[Philippians 2:v10-11]**..*

pp 93/183

REALITY *of* ***REALITY***

MOVEMENT NUMBER 3

Fixtures

Accept and follow the will of God for it is a fixture that can never die.

Cross-reference

FIXTURES

God does not change, He is not subject to anything, nothing at all can influence Him to be anything or anyway that He is not, this includes, time, energy, space feelings, free will, excuses absolutely there is nothing, something every person that ever was or is now or to come and all His creation should know as the first **fixture** in this entire creation, visible and touchable to the invisible and non touchable is the Almighty God and heavenly father,the creator of everything.. **Colossians 1: v16**.

Read

*For by Him all things were created, that are in heaven, and that are in earth, visible and invisible, whether they be thrones, or dominions, or principalities, or powers: all things were created by Him for Him.. **[Colossians 1:v16]**..*

Fixtures: are exactly that, **fixed** they cannot be changed, or removed all mankind are subject to them in this life and the next. This will be either a good thing or not depending on how people conduct themselves to the extent to see and acknowledge them or do not. These **Fixtures** are there in the everyday life, yet there are also **fixtures** in the salvation work of God.. Jesus is one **Fixture** that cannot be overlooked or bypassed, it is impossible to come to God without going through His son Jesus Christ.. **John 14:v6**..And his Gospel, in fact every word that proceeds from the mouth of God.. **Matthew 4:v4**..Another **Fixture** placed in the salvation plan of God is to hear and accept His servants active around the earth and in the spirit world, namely the true apostles first and those that they send and of

Cross-reference

course the others mentioned in holy scripture through their written testimonies.. and any other that God chooses to use, for God is no respecter of persons.. **Romans 2:v11**..He treats everyone with the same equal measure.

Read

*..[**John 14:v6**].. Jesus saith unto him, I am the way, the truth and the life: no man cometh unto the Father, but by me.. [**Matthew 4:v4**]..*
*But he answered and said, it is written. Man shall not live by bread alone, but by every word that proceeds out of the mouth of God... [**Romans2:v11**].. For there is no respect of persons with God..*

pp 152/ 235

Within this creation, created by the Almighty God are of course **fixtures**, these are found in the physical nature, yet also in the spiritual, they are really there, not all hidden and they can bring with them real consequences if ignored. **Now!!** Lets be reminded or unveil some everyday **fixtures** and what can happen if ignored Humans are Born as babies, grow up to adults it does not happen any other way, our spiritual birth growing up into maturity also takes time in a similar way, this happens as a person grows and develops through the power of the holy spirit together with our own spirit, onto maturity.. **John 3: v3.** Time is another **fixture** that man has no power over, moving onward always, putting everything behind it, measuring and timing everything ahead of it, still to come for there is both season and time.. **Ecclesiastes 3:v1**..

Read

*..[**John 3:v3**].. Jesus answered and said unto him, Verily, verily I say unto thee, except a man be born again, he cannot see the Kingdom of God.*

Cross-reference

Read *[Ecclesiastes3:v1]..To everything there is a season, and a time to every purpose under the heaven.*

Another **fixture**.. God created male and female in that order.. **Genesis 1:v27**..there is no other or in between, even with the interference of man's scientists and inherited sins of the fore fathers there will always be one dominating the other either male or female characteristics within that new little life, a true boy or true girl and be sure God knows and He will have the last say no matter what it seems, It would be down to the choice of that person should there be an inner tussle of feelings as to which sex is to be the dominant to ask Jesus for help, not seek your own way through doctors and scientists, but to know and do the will of God, not to enter into temptation and sin..

pp 40/65

Mark 10:v51..

Read *So God created man in His own image, in the image of God created he Him, male and female created He them..* ***[Genesis..1:v27]*.. .. *[Mark 10:v51]*..**
And Jesus answered and said unto him, what wilt thou that I should do unto thee.
Remember nothing is impossible (with) God.

Another **fixture** .. choice, every human being and person capable must choose to obey and worship God or the Devil Satan **Genesis..2:v16/17**..
Genesis 3:v4.. NO decision is not acceptable to God, He will rebuke such..
Revelation.. 3:v16..

pp 34/41/52

Cross-reference

Read

And the Lord God commanded the man, saying of every tree of the garden, thou mayest freely eat. But of the tree of the knowledge of good and evil, thou shalt not eat of it, for in the day thou eat thereof, thou shalt surely die.. ***[Genesis 2:v16-17]****..And the serpent said unto the woman, ye shat not surely die..*

pg 65

[Genesis 3:v4]*..* ***Read: all of chapter 3 for full knowledge and understanding.*** *So then*

pp 34/41/52

because thou art lukewarm, and neither cold nor hot, I will spew thee out of My mouth.. ***[Revelation 3:v16]..***

pg 213

Water and food, no one can survive without, the human brain and body has to be nourished, to grow and develop moving onto adulthood and maturity, each individual person must receive certain nutrients at regular intervals to live. This another known **fixture**. There is another **fixture**.. The soul and spirit or inner being, the non material self of every man needs also needs nourishment,**WORD OF GOD.. Matthew 4:v4**.. just as the creator talks to His visible creation, the weather, plants, tree animals insects, seeds and seasons etc, so that we have the natural substances for our bodies, that we as humans should have life, so too the word and spirit of God will feed us internally that we have life of His life.

Read

*..****[Matthew 4:v4]****..But he answered and said, it is written, Man shall not live by bread alone, but by every word that proceeds out of the mouth of God.*

Another **fixture**: Man has to now, because of the fall into sin, prove worthy of saving,

Cross-reference

and so Temptations are permitted by God yet do not come from Him, neither can He be tempted.. **Matthew 4: v7**. It is he that endures temptations that the man will be saved from entering into sin which is from the evil one.. **1 Corinthians 10:v13**..

Read

Jesus said unto him,It is written again, that thou shalt not tempt the Lord thy God.. ***[Matthew 4:v7]***.. *There hath no temptation taken you, but such as is common to man: but God is faithful, who will not suffer you to be tempted above that ye are able, but will with the temptation, also make a way to escape, that ye may be able to bear it..**[1 Corinthians 10:v13]**..*

The original early church established by Jesus Christ himself through his life, death and resurrection is a **fixture**, it cannot be copied nor replicated neither prevailed over by any evil force or power.. **Matthew 16: v18**..together with its chosen Apostle ministry, Christ words.. **Matthew 28: v19-20**.. and will last until the end of the world. God chooses

Read

And I say also unto thee, that thou art Peter, and upon this rock, I will build my church: and the gates of hell shall not prevail against it.. ***[Matthew16:v18]***.. ..

pp 175 /220 /186 /132

pp 158 / 184

[Matthew 28:v19-20]..*Go ye therefore and teach all nations, baptizing them, in the name of the Father, and of the son, and of the Holy Ghost. Teaching them to observe all things whatsoever I have commanded you: and, lo, I am with you always, even unto the end of the world. AMEN.*

Cross-reference

Another fixture.. certainly there are just too many mention.. God chooses He calls who and when.. ..**Ephesians 1::v4-5**

Read According as He has chosen us in Him, before the foundation of the world, that we should be Holy and without blame before Him in love: Having predestined us unto the adoption of children of Jesus Christ in himself according to the good pleasure of His will..***[Ephesians 4/5]***..

pg 196 One last **Fixture** brought out of my personal experiences: I give testimony that Gods word.. **Isaiah 55:v11**..Will return to Him having done what it said; everything will go back to the beginning or starting point,more examples a clock hands, the human body will return to the earth, sin and evil, go back to where it came from through the same path it came through, rain drops will return to the clouds, the earth rotates on its own axis to give us our calendar year, every year. **WHY? To give another opportunity to repent and be forgiven by the Lord.**

Read ***..[Isaiah 55:v11]..*** In your **okjb.**

NOTES

MOVEMENT NUMBER 4

Nature

Our nature either reflects the nature of God or the nature of the devil.

Cross-reference

NATURE

This is referring to God the creator, yet really just part of who He is, not Him in completeness, yet what constitutes His person and disposition, and us humans out of His lineage our descent, carry within us a part of that part we call nature giving everyone a portion of Godly personality and characteristic created in us to complement their physical and spiritual stature, to honor the Almighty God,..**Genesis 1: v27**..

Read *So God created man in His own image, in the image of God created he him,male and female created he them..[**Genesis 1:v27**]..*

pg 34

That's nature, the entire universe reflects the nature of the Almighty God, or to put another way, that which has come from and out of Him, yet this universe can not contain all He is.. **2 Chronicles 2: v6.**

Read *But who is able to build Him an house, seeing the heaven and heaven of heavens cannot contain him Who am I then, that should build Him an house?Save only to burn sacrifice unto Him..*
*..[**2 Chronicles 2:v6**]..*

This may seem unreal or not true, yet it is, even Satan the Devil and wicked one has the nature of God in him, yes because God had created Lucifer right from the start,yet a fallen angel.. **Isaiah 14v12**..for everything is made by Him.. **John 1:v3**

Read *How thou are fallen from heaven, Oh Lucifer, son of the morning ! how you are cut down to the ground, which did weaken the nations..*
*.. [**Isaiah14:v12**].*

pp 284 /177

Cross-reference

Read *.[John1:v3]..*
All things were made by Him; and without Him was not anything made that was made.

Each part big or small, with life and movement to each part still and non moving visible or invisible reveals something of the nature of the creator that humans can come to know Him, to know without compromise that He is alive, He exists. Yet the evil one Satan is out to oppose and destroy all that God is, even with the full knowledge that he cannot because God created him not the other way round Satan came out from God as a top angel, was given eternal life out of God's life, a free will to make his own choices and move around, intelligence and knowledge, yet because God is Holy, Righteous and truth cannot do evil or wrong neither sin that nature is reserved for the devil and those whom follow in that same nature. For more on God addressing the devil also known as the serpent, read: **Genesis chapter 3:v1-24**.. Some verses can be found in the bible segment below.

pp 34/35/52

Read **[Genesis** ***3:v1]***.. *Now the serpent was more subtle than the beast of the field, which the Lord God had made, and he said unto the woman, Yea hath God said, yea shall not eat of every tree of the garden?.. **[V4]**.. And the serpent said unto the woman, Ye shall not surely die..**[v14]**..And the Lord God said unto the serpent Because thou hast done this, thou art cursed above all cattle, and above every beast of the field thy belly shall thou go, and dust thou shall eat all the days of thy life..*

Cross-reference

Read

Read all verses from Genesis chapter three from your original king James bible.

And so this nature of God has standout characteristics that are not hidden yet not always easily recognized when the presence of the evil one is also nearby, the reason and why in this reality of reality movement he too is mentioned. The nature of God is selfless, all for the benefit of His creation, He has nothing to gain. Here are just a few examples of Gods spiritual nature in His physical creation for there is a lot of Godly providence going on that we don't just see because much of what is happening is taken for granted to name some,trees: offer shelter,food shelter, safety, a vantage point, for bird and animal life, wood for building, fire for cooking and warmth, paper for books provides information records, the sturdy Oak tree stands strong and tall pointing up to its maker, despite the ever changing weather, the tree has an array of shapes and colors to marvel at, to its life rings in its trunk that can tell how old it is, and how it has grown year on year, wide rings show good growth, narrow rings reflect slow, how it has to tap into the soil and nearby rivers with its root system to draw nutrients and water out from the earth and river, to reflect a the providence nature of its maker.

THE NATURE OF GOD IN THE EARTH

[Returning to mankind]

The nature within each one of us has the opportunity to live, grow and develop spreading out with the same nature and determination as

Cross-reference

the old oak tree in our above parable, when we convert the earthly story into a spiritual one. The diverse changing elements in the weather represent the evil one and his unrelenting attempts to bring down mankind, to destroy us by causing storms in our life that he hopes will stop us looking up to the heavens in prayer and work.. **Matthew 8: v24-27**. Keep focused on Jesus Christ.

Read

*And behold, there arose a great tempest in the sea, insomuch that the ship was covered with the waves: but he was asleep. And his disciples came to him, saying Lord save us: we perish. And he saith unto them, why are ye fearful, O ye of little faith, then he arose and rebuked the winds and the sea obeyed him.. [**Matthew 8:v24-27**]..*

It will be through determined actions together with the knowledge of the true nature of our loving God reflected in the life and character of Jesus Christ that will bring right naturally spoken words and works relating to faith in a life lived that reflects this one nature. Using the example of the great Oak tree, looking up to God both in words and actions, tapping into all the goodness from God that reflects in our life years.

NOTES

REALITY *of* ***REALITY***

MOVEMENT NUMBER 5

Everything Goes Back to the Beginning

Everything must return to where it came from, good or evil.

Cross-reference

EVERYTHING GOES BACK TO THE BEGINNING

God tries everything under the sun to save mankind from himself, time then becomes one of the Lord of Host's, to some time and events are just there because that is how it is or it is that way, yet there is so much more to it. God does not need time, He is time, with Him everything IS. Again we take to real examples to uncover this mystery of Gods love, the clock resting on the mantle piece in a home for the family to measure the different parts of the day and night, record events to the exact time and moment, as they will or have already happen, as they have been preplanned to take place, the clock itself goes back to the beginning after ticking for 24 hours or 1440 minutes 86400 seconds, no coincidence, days, weeks, months, years all go back to the beginning, to the starting point, seasons of sowing and harvesting feature year in year out, the earth rotates on its own axis, changing how the sun lights up the different parts or better said countries of the earth, to create days and nights, as this is happening giving making the year 365 1/4 days, once completed just to commence all over again, the sun also rotates on its axis taking 27 days to start all over again and again. Note!! "there

RR are two simultaneous events" ***Reality of Reality***. Always two. Let us now go to mankind to you and me, flesh and spirit, in these man was created, out of the dust of the ground.. **Genesis 2: v7**..and breathed into his nostrils the breath of life.

Cross-reference

Read

*And the Lord God formed the man of the dust of the ground, and breathed into his nostrils, the breath of life; and man became a living soul..**[Genesis 2:v7]**..*

In death the flesh will go back to where it came, the ground or into the earth, the spirit or breath of life will go back to the spirit world from where it also came Thus everything will go back to the beginning, even where it came from. So far the information recorded above is no secret to most learned grown up people, and has been written as a foundation for what is to follow, that may not be known to even the most prominent of persons in the high places including leaders of the seven churches.. **Revelation 1: v4** in Asia, where their teaching has since that time spread throughout the world.

Read

***JOHN** to the seven churches which are in Asia: Grace be unto you, and peace from him which is, and which was, and which is to come; and from the seven spirits which are before his throne.. **[Revelation 1:v4]**..*

RR

Everything will go back to the beginning : that's the ***reality of reality***. What transpires between being born and dying will in act these words for each soul conceived in the usual way, through sexual intercourse of a man and woman in marriage. During this in between period a struggle of life and a death ensues, a struggle between good and evil enacted out of righteous or wrongful actions, that God purposefully allows, this is where freedom of choice through choice joins the picture. Opportunities to temptations will be made available to

Cross-reference

pp 52 /101

everyone according to the will of God.. **Matthew 4:v1-11..**involving God through Jesus Christ, these offer a change of heart where a change of heart is required, temptations can re-emerge, where not resisted will cause the heart to harden harder and harder, we read about God hardening the heart of the Egyptian leader Pharaoh in the story:.. **Exodus 9:v12**..Pharoah wanted it his way and so God gave him what he wanted that is our loving God, He allows us what we want.

pg 196

Read

Then was Jesus led up of the spirit into the wilderness, to be tempted of the devil. And when he had fasted, forty days and forty nights, he was afterward an hungered. And when the tempter came to him, he said,if thou be the son of God Command that these stones be made bread. But he answered and said, it is written, man shall not live by bread alone, but every word that proceeds out of the mouth of God.. ***[Matthew 4:v1-4]****..Read till* ***verse 11*** *in your* ***OKJB***

Read

And the Lord hardened the heart of Pharaoh, and he hearkened not unto them, as the Lord had spoken unto Moses..
[Exodus 9:v12]*..*

Yet; when temptation to do evil has come, denying Jesus Christ "Lord" is evil too that same evil will return to its source the devil through the person/ persons it had manifest.. **James 4:v7**..It may be that at certain times that one has entered into wrong and evil actions or re-actions against or toward God and or a neighbor,

Cross-reference

after which at regular intervals by way of repeat opportunities the conscious will remind of any wrong doings, through choice by choice a change in response is made available, failing to do so will cause an increase of resistance to the gift of conscience simultaneously a decrease in the Godly image.

Read *Submit yourselves therefore to God, resist the devil, and he will flee from you..**[James 4:v7]..***

Recurring dreams bring about another opportunity to re visit our actions, for what happens in the flesh also effects the spirit.. **Job 33:v 15-18**. it is not out of the question; meeting up again with the wronged person in some way or other, to even returning to the same location as an opportunity to re-enact in the mind what took place,the offer of repentance by grace enabled by the Almighty God.

Read *In a dream, in a vision of the night, when deep sleep falls upon men, in slumbering upon the bed; Then he opened the ears of the men, and seals their instruction: That he may withdraw man from his purpose, and hide pride from man. He keeps back his soul from the pit, and his life from perishing from the sword.. **[Job 33:v15-18]**..*

NOTES

REALITY *of* ***REALITY***

MOVEMENT NUMBER 6

God's Love... What is it?

To speak God's love, one must feel the relief
out of Jesu Christ sacrifice of love

Cross-reference

GOD'S LOVE... WHAT IS IT?

God is love, love is God it says so in the first letter of John to congregations of the era and to everyone everywhere for all time periods..

1 John 4:v16.. Yet it is not just as simple as only saying it.. God loves you.. One has to know it to feel it by experience, even to spiritually touch it and how this happens is through His gracious acts of forgiveness through Jesus Christ sacrifice and the merit of it, boiling down to His word: **word of God = LOVE**.

Read

*And we have known and believed the love that God has to us. God is Love; and he that dwells in love, dwells in God, and God in him.. **[1 John 4v16]**..*

pg 169

Only by participating in the fullness of Jesus sacrifice on the cross with him, by way of a changed life style or a different focused life, a life reflecting the same to a life lived out close to Jesus life in following his, can one preach, teach, God loves you, because that person will have felt the relief provided for through the death of the cross, that relief is the release from the death grip of sin, the actual physical sacrificial death of Christ and the words, forgive them Father for they know not what they do.. **Luke 23:v34**.. Within the covers of the holy King James Bible where God is speaking his word: its love, aside where the devil has also had his say.. **Genesis 3:v1**..**Matthew 4:v9**.. its all God's voice, yet spoken through His servant or vessel.. **Joel chapter 1**..and by the donkey.. **Numbers 22:v28**..and of course God also speaks through His angels ..**Luke 2:v10**..

pp 34/35/41
pp 48 /101
pg 83

Cross-reference

Read *..[**Genesis 3:v1**]..You has God said, You shall not eat of every tree of the garden? And says unto him, all these things I will give thee, if you will fall down and worship me... [**Matthew4:v9**]..*

Read *[**Joel chapter 1:v1**]..The word of the Lord that came to Jo'el the son of Pe-thu-el and the Lord opened the mouth of the ass, and she said unto Ba'laam, what have I done unto thee, that thou has smitten me these three times.. [**Numbers..22:v28**].. And the angel said unto them, fear not: for, Behold I bring you good tidings of great joy, which shall be to all people..[**Luke 2:v10**]..*

pg 220

And because the Lord is Sovereign Lord.. His true image of goodness through creation does shine through in a few truthful words out of ordinary God fearing people. God is love reflected in and out of all His creation that is the heavens and earth the seen and touchable to the unseen and non touchable culminated when He joined in it fully in the incarnation of Jesus Christ appearing as both human and spirit, the flesh/the word that brought into this earthly realm real life flesh and blood examples what the love of God and God is love **(IS)** Peaking at the cross in the ultimate act of this serving love, the sacrifice of his own life offered in exchange for all the sins of mankind, shedding his innocent life and blood, he gave (served up) his life in victory, the life and death struggle came to its final conclusion for many on the cross that day.. **Matthew 20:v28..**not before though having spent his life living and walking with peoples from all walks of life, to visibly

Cross-reference

display this word **(LOVE)** The story of the good Samaritan.. **Luke 10 :v30-37**..

Read

pg 157

..***[Matthew 20:v28]***..*Even as I came not to be be ministered unto, but to minister, and to give his life a ransom to many..* ***[Luke 10:v30-37]..****And Jesus answering said; a certain man went down to Jerusalem to Jericho, and fell among thieves, which stripped him of his raiment, and wounded him, and departed, leaving him half dead. And by chance there came down a certain priest that way: and when he saw him, he passed by on the other side. And likewise a Levite, when he was at the place, came and looked on him, and passed by on the other side. But a certain Sa-mar'i-tan as he journeyed came where he was: and when he saw him, he had compassion on him. And went to him to bind up his wounds, pouring in oil and wine, and set him on his own beast, and brought him to an inn, and took care of him. And on the morrow when he departed, he took out two pence, and gave them to the host, and said unto him , Take care of him and whatsoever thou spends more, when I come again,I will repay thee. Which now of these three, thinks thou, was neighbor unto him, that fell among thieves ? And he said, he that showed mercy on him, Then said Jesus unto him, Go, and, do likewise..*

LOVE IN ACTION

Obedience to all that God is and commands by choice through choice ends it self to be good or suitable for this love.. **Mark 12: v30 -31** .. For Jesus said, Go and do likewise..

Cross-reference

Read

*..**[Mark 12: 30-31]**.. And thou shalt love the Lord thy God with all thy heart, and with all thy soul, and with all thy mind, and with all thy strength: this is the first commandment.*

The good Samaritan is none other than God in Jesus Christ going out of His way to pass through the earthly realm, this is the spirit or heart of God, the word. The beaten man is the soul and spirit of mankind hurt by the evil one. The Priest represents God the spirit in mankind that is blocked from doing right by flesh. The Levite represents the well to do mankind rich in worldly spirit. So far this parable is spiritual.. We carry on in the spirit. Now !! to love the Lord thy God with all thy heart and with all thy soul means: to be filled with the "word of God" with all thy strength means: in the ability to allow the word to do its work in us and through us, to recognize and resist the temptations by quenching the fiery darts of the evil one leading us to sin, which in effect opposition to this love.. **Ephesians 6:v16**..with all thy mind means: all that we consider, imagine understand plan and do, will first be born of the word of God in the resembling fashion as described above in Jesus Christ.

Read

*Above all, taking the shield of faith, wherewith ye shall be able to quench all the fiery darts of the wicked one..**[Ephesians 6:v16]**..*

pp 99/144

This love kind also produces corresponding feelings and affections, to be filled with this same sentiment God's love provides as described above within the confides of a marriage between a man and woman (husband and wife) are truly

Cross-reference

felt when there is also the intimacy presence of Jesus Christ.

RR In this ***Reality of Reality*** I mention nothing about the other love, the love that the devil offers, a love that opposes the love of God, the love for money, the root of all kinds of evils..**1 Timothy 6:v10**.. This love is

RR brought to the ***Reality of Reality*** in (book 2)

Read *For the love of money is the root of all evil, which while some coveted after, they have erred from the faith, and have pierced themselves through with many sorrows..* ***[1 Timothy 6:v10*** **]..**

REALITY *of* ***REALITY***

MOVEMENT NUMBER 7

Unity

Only through unity in Jesus Christ will give us unity in everything else.

Cross-reference

UNITY

It is no surprise neither a mystery to conclude that the visible creation of the universe work together as does the designer and maker Himself to continuously reform itself through a diverse network of living organisms, creatures, planets the moon and sun producing life giving sustaining elements for this purpose of reflecting a unified creator, a God that is one with what He says, whom He is to what He does, He is also one with those whom are one with Him, Jesus His only begotten son and the Holy Ghost, they all agree as one, there is no confusion to be found in and with the Lord God, yet confusion and disunion between God and man has been lost due to the creeping in of the evil one offering an alternative choice for man to choose, than the Lord, that came by way of lies and confusion..

.. **Genesis chapter 3**.. from your bible refer to **chapter 8**.

God consists of three persons in one, known as the triune God or Godhead. **(1)** God the Father, He is the Father figure of all father"s yet he is in the spiritual. **(2)** God the son Jesus Christ, he is the word that took on flesh and blood, Jesus is the exact image of his Father in the words that he spoke and did. **(3)** God the Holy Spirit or Holy Ghost.. this Holy Spirit is able to join to the spirit of a person or mankind.

pp 111 /198

Read *For there are three that bear record in heaven, the Father, the word, and the Holy Ghost: and these three are one.. **[1 John 5:v7]**..*

Man also consists of three parts, **(1)** spirit, **(2)** Soul, **(3)** body and these three are to be in complete unity, Yet often not, why ? Because of choice, he is free to choose, whom to obey, God or Devil,

Cross-reference

often mixing with both causing disunion within himself, for the spirit is willing but the flesh is not, or the words say one thing but inside something else is going on.. If you know what I mean ?..**1 Thessalonians 5:v23**..

Read *And the very God of peace sanctify you wholly; and I pray God your whole spirit soul and body, be preserved blameless, until the coming of our Lord Jesus Christ..[**1 Thessalonians 5:v23**]..*

pg 113

Man was given the commission to take care of the creation even to the point of having dominion (reign over or take control of) to naming every living creature.. **Genesis 1:v28, Genesis 2:v20**.. God calling out unity between man and beast.

Read *.. [**Genesis1:v28**]..And God blessed them, God said unto them, be fruitful and multiply, and replenish the earth, and subdue it: and have dominion over the fish of the sea, and over the fowl of the air, and over every living thing that moves upon the earth. ..[**Genesis 2:v20**].. (part) And Adam gave names to all cattle, and to the fowl of the air, and to every beast of the field..*

Yet because of sin and entry into the physical earth by the evil one, unity had been broken in all areas, Man and God, Man and Man, Man and animals/creatures, yet God was not about give up on mankind the crown of His creation and so devised a plan to send one, whom He would use to restore all lost unities,Jesus Christ.. **1 Corinthians 15:v28**.. despite everything that would come to pass..

pg 74

Read *And when all things shall be subdued unto Him, then shall the son also himself be subject unto*

Cross-reference

Read *him, that put all things under him, that God may be all in all...[**1 Corinthians 15:v28**]..*

Imagine giving a family member an opportunity to use and take care of your one prize possession, to enjoy in his properties yet look well after it only to watch it get disrupted, torn apart, that's the real picture merging out of selfish, greedy power hungry MANKIND, that often leaves neighbors destitute or dead. For me, the author, In my personal capacity see nothing worse decaying than a mind that thinks one thing yet the tongue says something else, a character that portrays one type, yet reveals a different one, an evil heart that hides behind a good facade, one pretending to be someone that they are not, hiding behind pretentious acts, seemingly right actions yet wrong, their intentions and end result is for no other purpose than selfish ill gotten personal gain or satisfaction, bringing with it confusion. God looks at the heart, not outward appearance for it is out of an evil heart that disobeys and dishonors Him, yet a pure heart that God can rescue and use to save others..**1 Samuel 16: v7.. Matthew 5: v8**..

Read *..[**1 Samuel 16:v7**]..But the Lord said unto Samuel,Look not on his countenance, or on the height of his stature; because I have refused him: for the Lord sees not as man sees; for man looks on the outward appearance, but the Lord looks on the heart.. [**Matthew 5:v8**].. For the pure in heart will see God.*

pg 143

I tell the truth, that persons even Christians behaving this way will be caught out speedily by the Triune God, whom is Himself is

Cross-reference

the perfection of unity, He enlightens man with these simple words, But Let your communication be Yea, yea; Nay nay.. For whatsoever is more than these cometh of evil.. ..**Matthew 5:v37**.. Anyone that is not one with themselves cannot be one with their own families friends, neither with his neighbors, not with the Lord, his life can end sorrowful in disorientation and fear. To unite yourself with yourself, the **first step** one has to choose to do is to unite with God, for He is the power, the authority over confusion, this happens by the accepting Jesus Christ as the link or go between man and God.. **John 14 :v6**. Because nothing happens instantly and because it has taken time to come to this moment, the same is needed to reverse the position, through persistent striving, driven by the want to change and with the help of God through His son Jesus Christ in His Gospel word and prayer as is preserved in the books of the original King James bible. this ***Reality of Reality*** book is compiled as an addition for ease of understanding in the application of this Bible, yet one should acquire this bible which covers the words and actions of the Lord.

RR

Read

*..**[John 14:v6]**.. Jesus said unto him, I am the way, the truth, and the life: no man cometh unto the Father by Me..*

The **second step** after accepting and choosing to enact the first step in this process of undoing what has been wrongfully done is to cast out these wrongs by inputting righteousness, making the word of God into both a speaking and a doing way of life.. **John 1:v1**.. in so doing the

Cross-reference

power and authority of the the Lord your God will not just cast out all confusion that comes from the evil one, He will set you on the right course to unite with yourself but also with all of His creation visible and invisible, it will be a trip through the Kingdom of God on earth, amidst all the worldly wicked deeds of those on the outside.

Read

In the beginning was the Word, and the word was with God, and the word was God..
***[John 1:v1]**..*

For God is not the author of confusion, but of peace, as in all the churches of the saints..**1 Corinthians 14:v33**

REALITY *of* ***REALITY***

MOVEMENT NUMBER 8

There Has to Be a Right Way

Right / Right equals right outcome.
Wrong / Wrong equals wrong outcome.
Right / Wrong equals wrong outcome.

Cross-reference

THERE HAS TO BE A RIGHT WAY

In the Kingdom of God there was the triune God together with His Angels created to serve Him freely, this information is as lean as it gets for it would not be right to speak more than is really known. Beginning with the Kingdom it is right to say that as long as the angels freely obeyed God they could remain, they would be taken care of, have need of nothing, would surely never be cast out neither die, it is right to say then that Gods way is the right way and if this way was to continue there would not be any other way. Something changed though, something went horribly wrong that set in motion not just another way a very broad wide way that continues to get wider.. Man has the freedom to choose: Gods narrow right way or the broad wrong way, the narrow right way will lead to God and life, whereas the broad wrong way will lead to the devil and death.. **Matthew 7:v13**..

Read

*Enter ye in at the strait gate: for wide is the gate and broad is the way, that leads to destruction, and many there be which go in thereat. Because strait is the gate,and narrow is the way, which leads unto life, and few there be that find it..**[Matthew 7:v13-14]**..*

There is in everything said and done a right way.. yet so many wrong ways.

God does not change, He can never be anything other than who He is, and so had to let some of the self seeking angels go on their own way, casting them out of the Kingdom to become vagabond spirits beings roaming around in

Cross-reference

time and space, these vagabond spirits are the broad way and are around. So what was the creator to do about this situation, after all He is a creator and so had future plans to fill His creation with new things with a family to love and take good care of, well because our God knows everything even before ahead of it happening would not look back on these plans, yet set them in motion at the right time of course Those plans included creating a physical universe with physical beings, we now know as mankind having their own free will just like the angels and so we carry on the story from the perspective of the Holy scriptures starting with of course

Read **Genesis 1.. in your original king James bible** Having put the finishing touches to His static physical universe creation, it had reached the right time to put some life in it.. **Genesis 1: v26**.. and re affirm that right way too.. **Genesis 2: v17..in these examples I add that included in the right way is also at the right time,** with God everything comes together right and perfect.

pg 34
pg 35

Read *But of the tree of knowledge of good and evil, thou shalt not eat of it: for in the day that thou eat thereof, thou shalt surely die..* ***[Genesis 2:v17]***..

The consequences of going about things in the wrong way, are disastrous to say the least, as told in the right bible chapters and verses as given in the Read paragraphs.

All was going right in this new physical creation or so it seemed, yet danger was lurking in the midst, the fallen spiritual Angels including the instigator or head Angel, known as Lucifer...

Cross-reference

Ezekiel 28: v16.. would offer the other way, his broad way to the unsuspecting new life beings Adam and Eve tempting them with lies and deceit to disobey God, bringing with it a life and death struggle that continues to this day.. **Revelation 12:v7-9**..

Read

*..**[Ezekiel 28:v16]**..By the multitude of thy merchandise, they have filled the midst of thee with violence,and thou hast sinned: therefor I will cast as profane out of the mountain of God: and I will destroy thee, O covering cherub, from the midst of the stones of fire.*

Read

*And there was war in heaven: Michael and his angels fought against the Dragon and the dragon fought and his angels. And prevailed not: neither was their place found in heaven.. **[Revelation 12:v7-9]**..*

The struggle for life is to remain with God and on the right way, that means to say and do what is right always not shifting, this is called righteousness, by faith Abraham was righteous in the sight of God..
Romans 4:v3.When we obey the word of God by action it will always be right.
The broad way is where anything goes, certainly God is in this way, no rules a total disregard for anything right or righteous living, this way is the way of the foolish,a complete opposite to the righteous and will lead to a self destructive life that will often swell over to family and friends and total separation from an all loving God, that just cannot be involved in anything wrong.

Cross-reference

Read

For what says the scripture? Abraham believed; God, and it was counted unto him for righteousness.. ***[Romans 4:v3]***..

Certainly there are rewards for striving and doing right, God would not be the righteous God He is if our efforts in Him were not recognized, would He ? This righteous God continues from here on in this same style and manner, not in any way changing going on to compile centuries of history under one cover of the Holy bible, mysteries of the Kingdom of God revealed, super natural inexplicable wonders and miracles performed, truths explained through action, God the word coming to life in the flesh of Jesus Christ, all this to reveal and make known that there is the one right way. We conclude this chapter touching on how the right way has been set into the future and plan of God to rid the creation of the broad way once and for all. God has set apart His own as a family, for this He has set Himself up as, Father, a right church as a mother, right and chosen ordained servants to carry out His will in this.

NOTES

REALITY *of* ***REALITY***

MOVEMENT NUMBER 9

Free Will

Whatsoever the outcome of our lives, we have free willed it that way.

Cross-reference

FREE WILL

Out of the nature of God, being himself free willed answering to no other, created He: Angels and Humans, also with a free will, what this amounts too, the ability to choose a path to follow, to make choices freely, without being forced, or coerced in anyway, not through fine or punishment, this is within the loving God an unfathomable love, God will not interfere with that free will, until that free by an individual has been given back to Him, by choice through choice, yet giving or allowing whatsoever is wanted, amidst having only thoughts and plans of prosperity towards that person, not to harm, plans to give hope and a future.. **Jeremiah 29:v11**..Having a free will forms part of that image of God in man

Read *For I know the thoughts that I think toward you,saith the Lord, thoughts of peace and not of evil, to give you an expected end.. **[Jeremiah 29:v11]**..*

pg 202

And so!! God does not just interfere without a consent or a pleading (prayer) out of which He will intervene for the good often rebuking and or blocking the evil one at that time from doing harm to a soul crying out for divine help, trying even to change their life and the hope of being saved after coming to the realization the path they are on is not the right one. Changing ones original will, choice or way of life can be a good thing, it can be that the Almighty God intervenes by showing Himself, here is an example where He did just that.. **Acts 9:v1-43.. Acts 13:v9**..

pp 71/ 213

Cross-reference

Read *And as he journeyed, he came near Damascus, and suddenly there shined round about him a light from heaven. And he fell to the earth, and heard a voice saying unto him, Saul, Saul, why persecute thou me ? And he said, who art thou Lord ? and the Lord said, I am Jesus whom thou persecutes: It is hard for thee to kick against the pricks. And he trembling and astonished said, Lord what wilt thou have me to do? And the Lord said unto him. Arise and go into the city, and it shall be told thee, what thou must do..* ***[Acts 9:v3-6]..READ***

Read ***ALL THE CHAPTER:..[Acts13:v9]..*** *Then*

pp 70/ 213 *Saul (who is also called Paul)*

In the story or Saul whom later became Paul, Jesus changed the path or direction of his life, from a life that opposed Jesus, to a life that followed Jesus, a life that if he had continued with,would have destroyed himself. Jesus was able to change Saul way of thinking and believing that he did an about turn completely and from that time onward, Saul the now Paul spent the rest of his serving those that he once persecuted.

The events of everyday life, all around and about us people are holding under their control at the blink of an eye the choice to do good or evil that will reflect the same consequences for themselves, their family friends and neighbors behaving the way that they want and choose.

pp 164 / 141 Nations, governments and world leaders have inflicted all kinds of atrocities with their ability of this free will.. **Matthew 24:v6**..

Read *And ye shall hear of wars and rumors of wars, see that ye be not troubled, for all these things*

Cross-reference

Read *must come to pass, but the end is not yet..* ***[Matthew 24:v6]..***

When analyzing these few words in less sentences, it becomes clear why the world is in the state it is.. **FREE WILL**.. A loving gift given from a loving God, has returned to the creator like a voice echoing in the wilderness..
John 1: v23..

Read *He said I am the voice of one crying in the wilderness, make straight the way of the Lord, as said the prophet E-sa-ias..* ***[John 1:v23].. A call to repent or change.***

Free will, that is freedom of choice, the gift of love by the giver God,is the cause for the contamination of sin, bringing with it the sorrows, pain and death. God had a plan to complete His kingdom, but because of free will, He has chosen to create the earthly realm as we know it today, incorporating the universe to finish what He has started, God will always have the first and the last say, He is the Alpha and Omega.. **Revelation 22:v13**..

Read *I am Alpha and Omega, the beginning and the end, the first and the last..* ***[Revelation 22:v13]..***

pp 74/161

Jesus uses a story, a parable; how and who will be involved in His plan to put an end to free will by choice through choice.. The Almighty Lord God is pictured as a King, this King has a son Jesus Christ, this king wants to find a suitable virgin bride for his only son, this bride is made up of many individual persons from all over the world, out from amongst the nations of the earth, from all walks of life; either the poor or rich clever or ignorant,

Cross-reference

is not what counts, the big or small in stature God the king gives NO favor, the status of royalty, the kings, queens, governors of the earth are not what this King of Kings is looking for, HE particularly looks at the heart, those that hear the proposal of marriage and be part of the unique virgin bride for His son and have made themselves worthy for the groom, by becoming spiritually pure and ready, the image of a virgin bride yet made up of many out of all the nations of the world, these are those persons that have followed Jesus Gospel giving back their free will to do so that has gone out to whole world.

pg 17

To illustrate this: Jesus uses a parable, an earthly story with an heavenly (spiritual) meaning, telling of ten virgins, (worthy *t*o marry) five wise and five foolish however five did not make themselves ready and five did, five represents a larger number.. **Matthew25:v1-13**..

And so many will be called but few will be chosen. Read the full parable in your

Read **OKJB. ..[Matthew 25:v1-13]**

Going hand in hand with the parable of the Ten virgins and the bride of Christ, the preparation work as with a natural marriage there is planning and preparation, God the King has called His servants these are ordinary men and women from among the nations societies to carry out this preparation work both in the physical and spiritual form, certain men have been called and ordained into specific ministerial tasks for this to which they have given their yes, yes and no, no too.. this is where the church of Christ becomes the image God has created to separate from the worldly work.

The absolute plan of the Almighty God is to take

Cross-reference

back free will by choice through choice, this then forms part of this plan when those accept the call and give it over, obey and follow the the Lamb of God (His son Jesus) wherever He goes.. **Revelation 14:v14**..

Read *These are they which were not defiled with women; for they are virgins. These are they which follow the lamb, whither soever he goes These were redeemed from among men, being the first fruits unto God unto the lamb.* ***..[Revelation 14:v14]..***

Two choices linked into one, in doing so the reward will be with the Lord, those whom refuse to give back their free will and freedom of choice, their reward is also is with the Lord whom will reward them accordingly along with their free will in the choices they have made and lived by.. **Revelation 22: v12**..

Read *And, behold I come quickly and My reward is with me, to give every man according as his work shall be..* ***[Revelation 22:v12]***..

pg 72

The entire universe and everything it contains the heavens and the earth, have been created for this single purpose of free will, after which a new heaven and a new earth ushered in.. **Revelation 21:v1-3**..in other words ..

pg 145 A brand new creation, (as the saying goes) designed and built on one will, no more choices, and God will be all in all, through Jesus His son, for all and for all and eternity.. **1 Corinthians 15:v28**..

pg 59 Read *..**[1 Corinthians 15:v28]**..And when all things shall be subdued under him, then shall the son also himself be subject unto him, that put all things under him that God may be all in all.*

REALITY *of* ***REALITY***

MOVEMENT NUMBER 10

A Life Focussed on the Earthly Life

The same life lived on earth will be the same life lived after death in the grave.

Cross-reference

A LIFE FOCUSSED ON THE EARTHLY LIFE

After this life; the first life, or earth life, there is another life, the second life or spiritual life, dying and the grave are not the end, just the end of the life in the physical, the end of the flesh body, the body that houses the essence of the life of a person. This spirit life is to live on returning to the spirit world, heaven from where it came out of, at this transition a new out of the flesh body opportunity is opened up to those whom had been hurt, abused, killed or disadvantaged that occurred whilst living in this first life, even to suffering.. **Luke 16:v19-31**..

Read

*..**[Luke 16:v19-31]**..There was a certain rich man, which was clothed in purple and fine linen, and fared sumptuously every day:And there was a certain beggar named which was laid at his gate, full of sore. And desiring to be fed with the crumbs that fell from the rich mans table: moreover the dogs came and licked his sores, and it came to pass, that the beggar died, and was carried by the angels into Abraham's bosom: the rich man also died and was buried. And in hell he lifted up his eyes, being in torments, and sees Abraham from afar of, and Lazarus in his bosom, and he cried and said father Abraham, have mercy upon me, and send Lazarus that he may dip his finger In water,and cool my tongue; for I am tortured in this flame. But Abraham said son, remember that thou in thy lifetime received thy good things and likewise Lazarus evil things, but he is comforted and thou art tormented.*

pp 169 /26 /25 /245

Cross-reference

What this parable teaches: those who neither strove for earthly fame or fortune OR complained about their situation, having not heard of or known Jesus Christ the way the truth and the life through no fault of their own in the first life, now can get to know this Jesus Christ, learn of and follow this way and truth going on to accept him as their Saviour.. **Romans 10:v9**.. released from the flesh body, free of their oppressors, will become the advantaged and rewarded with inner peace.

Read *That if thou shalt confess with thy mouth the Lord Jesus, and shalt believe in thine heart that God hath raised him from the dead, thou shalt be saved.. **[Romans 10:v9]**..*

As for the advantaged, the worldly rich, to those whom knew Jesus Christ as Christians even the prominent the same process of reward applies, yet for this group it could mean that what was an advantage in the first life simply because the essence of that person was in the flesh or mammon.. **Matthew 6: v24**.. now puts them at a disadvantage in the second or spirit life, where none or not enough concern for this second life had been considered.. **Matthew 6: 19-21**.

Read *..**[Matthew 6:v24]**.. No man can serve two masters: for either he will hate the one and love the other; or else he will hold to the one, and despise the other, Ye, can not serve God and mammon.. **[Matthew 6:v19-21]**.. Lay not up for yourself treasures upon the earth, where moth and rust doth corrupt, and where thieves break through and steal: but lay up for yourself treasures in heaven, where neither moth nor*

pp 241 / 228 /181 /293

Cross-reference | Read

rust, does corrupt, and where thieves do not break through and steal.

Pausing for a moment: Clearly there are two possible endings coming out of this life, the end is determined by focus, a life focused on the things of the flesh to have more of the world, OR a life focused on the things spiritual, yet the one can not be separated from the other, the world of physical and the world of the spiritual live simultaneously, until in the grave where a split will take place, a bit like a split in an earthly built road where out of one lane, what seems to be no way forward, a turn to the right, a turn to the left will be shown or directed by an angel of the Lord, for the individual having chosen a life focused on Jesus, the angel of life will direct the now soul and spirit to the place he will go too, the other one who chose a life focused on the worldly, not noticing Jesus, the angel of death will direct the now soul and spirit to the place he will go too and remain. To understand this as a picture of life, it is a journey moving from one place to another, obviously when this does happen in real life, going to settle in another place, perhaps a country, treasured goods and possessions are shipped on or taken with and so too it's the same here, both of these will have something waiting for them: going to the right, the treasures of freedom, peace and life, treasures that came out of accepting and the following Jesus Christ, through the bible and his gospel message and servants.. **Matthew 10:v40**.. OR those having focused on the things earthly, will have no treasures stored up and waiting for them, for this group, it will be a place like a

Cross-reference

prison no freedom, darkness, cold scary,no life, evil will be experienced perpetually, for some in this group hatred will be the driving force, the spirit that was served on earth.

Read

*..[**Matthew 10:v40**].. He that receives you receives me, and he that receives me receives Him that sent me...words of Jesus Christ about his Father in heaven, having sent him and he in turn having sent his servants, who are active on earth.*

The life in the next life is mirrored by the earth life, there are buildings, cars and roads, hills and valleys, people ,prisons, churches everything that is in this first life is in the second life, the difference being nothing can be touched it is not a physical realm or place, its spiritual people are spirits in a soul, even the altar that represents the life, sacrificial death and resurrection to eternal life of Jesus Christ is there.. **Revelation 6:v9**..

Read

*..[**Revelation 6:v9**]..And when he had opened the fifth seal, I saw under the altar the soul's that were slain for the word of God, and for the testimony which they held.*

pg 183

So the flesh body will go back to the earth, where it came from, having served its purpose and cause, a temple for its life of the souls and spirit.

NOTES

REALITY *of* ***REALITY***

MOVEMENT NUMBER 11

Bibles

Having a bible does not constitute or mean owning the Holy Bible However God / Jesus Christ the word remains Holy.

Cross-reference

BIBLES

Under this heading, I am referring specifically to the adding to the removing, of singular to a collection of or linked words, phrases, chapters, verses to wittingly compiling a different named bible version for reasons of personalizing, self gain purpose or reason, not having been authorized to do so by the author and owner the Almighty God, who warns against such action.. **Revelation 22:v18/19**..

Read

For I testify unto every man that hears the words of the prophecy of this book. If any man shall add unto these things, God shall add unto him the plagues that are written in this book: And if any man shall take away from the words of the book of this prophecy, God shall take away his part out of the holy city, and from the things which are written in this book.. ***[Revelation 22:v18/19]***..

The original King James holy bible made up of its 66 old and new testament books and the Apocrypha which has 15 more smaller books, has been inspired and compiled through the super natural enacting of the holy spirit on and off during the history of the physical earth by individuals and families, nations and peoples telling about their personal encounters and inspirations, the wonders and miracles witnessed at the direct commanding word pronounced by God over the elements of nature, which includes over the animal kingdom.. **Numbers 22:v28**.. God showing He has total control.. **Exodus 14:v2**..

Cross-reference
pg 52

Read

***[Numbers 22:v28]**.. And the Lord opened the mouth of the ass,and she said unto Balaam, What have I done unto thee, that thou has smitten me, these three times.. **[Exodus 14:v21]**.. And Moses stretched out his hand over the sea; and the Lord caused the sea to go back by a strong east wind all that night, and the waters were divided.*

The Holy Bible is made Holy when it is set apart for Gods use, so if the bible that you have in your possession has been tampered with for the wrong reason and use could be miss leading, by the changing of God's spoken words its likely to produce the complete wrong message, the words in the original king James holy bible are God Himself put into ordinary people to speak and live by what they say later for the same word to come to life in **Jesus Christ** having been born into this very existence to expose and separate good and evil, life and death brought out of the words as recorded,for Jesus is the word and the word is Jesus.. **John 1:v14** it is the word that directs and illuminates our strait path that will lead us to enter through the narrow gate.. **Psalm 119:v105**.. A bit like an illuminated road sign that always point the way to ones desired destination even in the dark or at night and so one wrong word or dull sign can direct away from entering this strait gate.. **Matthew 7:v13/14**.. Most assuredly with introduction of more and

RR

more tampered with bibles, the; ***reality of reality***, if one is going to have a bible, have the right one, owning a bible doesn't mean its Holy.. **Yet God's word remains Holy.**

Cross-reference

Read *[John 1:v14]..and the word was made flesh, and dwelt among us,(and we beheld his glory, the glory as of the only begotten of the Father,) full of grace and truth.* ***[Psalm 119:v105]****..thy word is a lamp unto my feet, and a light unto my path.. Enter ye in at the strait gate: for wide is the gate, and broad is the way that leads to destruction, and many there be which go in thereat..* ***[Matthew 7:v13]****..because strait is the gate, and narrow is the way, which leads unto life, and few there be that find it..* ***[v14]****.*

When one is serious, has the right intentions to learn something new, from the starting point choosing the right tools and equipment is vital, the best teacher even a master will be the treasures to success after having recognized the call into something that will mean a continued participating, in a struggle through hardship and work to gain success, with these tools: to separate oneself from the world and evil to be Holy.. **1 Peter 1: 15-16**.. The one calling has the right tools.

Read *..[****1 Peter 1:v15-17****]..But as he which have called you is holy, so ye be holy in all manner of conversation; Because it is written, be ye holy; for I am holy.*

I recommend the original King James Bible with Apocrypha, there is available also a version that includes the book of Enoch for the dedicated reader, either untouched version from around the early 1611 time will be good enough, the shear intensity with which this bible had been translated and put together is in itself a wonder, a mystery revealed of Gods love and commitment

Cross-reference

to rescue mankind from the prophesies recorded, by providing and preserving His one true nature, He is the word and the word is Him, surely the Father of all Fathers yet in the heavenly places, the Alpha and Omega the beginning and the end of everything that was and is to come.. **Revelation 1:v8**..

Read

*..[**Revelation 1:v8**].. I am Alpha and Omega, the beginning and the ending, saith the Lord, which is, and which was, and which is to come, the Almighty.*

pg 171

The above does not include bibles written in other languages, translated from the original tongues, Hebrew and Greek into the worlds roughly 7117 different spoken languages as at 2021, though some of those known languages may only be used by a handful of that particular remaining tribe, should a holy bible ever been printed for them, it should be accurately translated, for this is a promise made by God.. **Mark 16:v15**..No one is to be forgotten neither left out. The Bible relates a true story of love, love exemplified by its words, words that are the essence of all love is and can ever be, these words come to life through what they say.. **John 1:v14**..It is these words that will never die, beyond this earthly life, the universe, the heavens or spirit realms, this word of God will remain, it will continue to speak, continue to live, no other kind of power or force will be able to silence what and when it wills to speak. The story of love is the true and basic message of the old and new testaments of the bible dealing with the physical nature of creation in the Old Testament and the spiritual

pp 117 /145

Cross-reference

in the New Testament, combining them into one thought the life death and resurrection of Jesus Christ, who is the true God.. **1John1:v1**..and true man.. **Philippians 2:v7**..

Read

*..**[Mark16:v15]**..And He said unto them, Go you into all the world, and preach the gospel to every creature.. **[1 John1:v1]**.*
*THAT..Which was from the beginning, which we have heard, which we have seen with our eyes, which we have looked upon, and our hands have handled, of the word of life..**[Philippians 2:v7]**.. But made himself of no reputation, and took upon him the form of a servant and was made in the likeness of men..*

REALITY *of* ***REALITY***

MOVEMENT NUMBER 12

Prayer

Prayers are a gift and covenant agreement.

Cross-reference

PRAYER

This type of gift from God is open to everyone, no restrictions, no rituals nor predetermined rules or qualifications are required or necessary before talking to the Almighty God.

Praying to God is a privilege, not a problem it enhances the believer's faith.

Prayer is the principle of faith, to believe that God is there that He does exist to talk too, because our physical and mental faculties does not show that God is there, our spiritual faculty of faith will do that to the point when He is felt, to the point where He can almost be touched.

When praying to God it is a personal encounter God is someone and not just something, actually people are made out of His image and likeness.

Therefore communication is in us because it is first in Him.

Where there is speaking there is listening and hearing, God hears when we pray, He is not restricted to one individual but hears all prayers from all people at the same time.

We come a little closer to receiving what we have requested when we believe that now God has heard and listened to our prayer for help that He will also respond or act.

Certainly when speaking to God it will not be a one-way conversation, He is going to respond albeit in His time.

Believing that God can and will make things happen that He can use people and things for His purpose that He is in control of His creation, nothing is impossible with Him, and God will give what is asked for.

Without any doubt, without any forcing of the faith, stimulate it rather by listening to answers to prayers, by reading the scriptures.

Cross-reference

And so a sound prayer must have faith and trust behind it, believing that God does really exist..**Proverbs3:5**.. It s completely needed that the prayer is driven by a child like disposition, one of supplication and thanksgiving..

Not knowing things or reasons why, yet trusting in God through a sound faith, can change the situation..**Philippians4:v6-7**.
once the requests are made known to God, there will be a period of waiting, one is to exercise patience and not get anxious, God knows what these requests are even before we do before the prayer.. **Matthew 6:v8..** for he has
pp 204/294
already taken any need to heart, He will already have a way forward even where there seems to be no way.

Read ***..[Proverbs 3:v5]..*** *Trust in the Lord with all your thine heart; and lean not unto thine own understanding..*
pp 921 /128 /262
..[Philippians 4:v6-7]..
Be anxious (careful) for nothing; but in everything by prayer and supplication with thanksgiving let your requests be made known to God. And the peace of God, which surpasses all understanding shall keep your hearts and minds through Christ Jesus. ***..[Matthew 6:v8]..****Be not ye therefore like unto them: for your Father knows what things ye have need of, before ye ask him..*
pg 198

Read ***THE LORD'S PRAYER:***
Our Father who is in heaven, hallowed be thy name, thy kingdom come thy will be done on earth as it is in heaven, give us this day our daily bread, .

The result of a sincere prayer, that is to pray in the mind and spirit of God as did Jesus when he said at the end of his most difficult prayer

Cross-reference

knowing what was about to happen to him.. **NOT MY WILL BUT THINE BE DONE.. Luke 22:v42**..I have learned that praying in the negative sense as described here, that no matter the outcome the peace that Jesus gives remains, an heard prayer leaves one feeling totally at peace.. convinced that where there seems no way God will make a way. .**Isaiah 43 v19**..

Read

..*[**Luke 22:v42**]..Saying, Father, If thou be willing ? Remove this cup from me: nevertheless not my will, but thine, be done..* ***[Isaiah 43:v19]**..Behold. I will do a new thing; now it shall spring forth; shall ye not know it? I will even make a way in the wilderness, and rivers in the desert..*

Prayers of the individual, for the individual or for and on behalf of others, are to be born out of the desires of the one praying and with the right faith, meaning with the corresponding bible word.. **Romans 10:v8.**.and action.. **James 2:v17** When there is a strong enough bond between persons so much so that the one having the stronger faith and knowing the plight of the other or others, through searching holy scripture will be able to bring the corresponding bible verse to the Lord in a resounding out loud sincere heart rendered prayer, in doing so the Lord will not go against Himself, He will carry out His own words to action for the circumstance to be removed, the same applies to the collective prayer taught by Jesus, when a congregation or when two or three gather in Jesus name to pray the **Our Father** as it is known,the prayer that the Lord gave to unite his disciples into

Cross-reference

one fellowship.. **Matthew 6:v9**..Which becomes a joint powerful rendition to the creator, the significance is that it was brought directly out of the teaching of Jesus Christ specifically for the church or body of believers, and through an active faith of patience in the Lord, nothing will be impossible.. **Matthew 20:v7**..

pg 126

Read ..*[**Romans 10:v8**]..But what saith it? The word is nigh thee, even in thy mouth and in thy heart: that is, the word of faith, which we preach.. [**James 2:v17**]..Even so faith, if it hath not works, is dead, being alone.. [**Matthew 6:v9**].. Our Father which art in heaven, Hallowed be thy name, Thy kingdom come, Thy will be done in earth as it is in heaven. Give us this day our daily bread. And forgive us our debts, as we forgive our debtors. And lead us not into temptation, but deliver us the evil one: for thine is the kingdom, and the power, and the glory, for ever Amen.*

God wants mankind to get to know Him for who He is, Loving, Faithful and Truth He does not have to prove Himself neither does He have show His power, but willing, and so He has given this gift of Prayer to the faithful believer, to use for the good of those who love Him, the essence of which this Almighty power can be unleashed to make the impossible, with God.. possible.. **Mark 10:v27**..

Read ..*[**Mark10:v27**].. And Jesus looking upon them saith, With men it is impossible, but with God all things are possible..*

Cross-reference

I have briefly covered two types of prayer, the individual, the collective, both of which are powerful in their own right, yet a prayer brought out of the Holy Spirit is guaranteed to have eternal life saving elements.. **Romans 8**..Prayers out of the Holy Ghost are the utterances of God,He alone knows what is needed for the eternal, the life in the spirit, the future.. **Matthew 10:v20**..Prayer is not made perfect using vain repetitions and much speaking, yet are by short precise and believing ones specific to the cause.. **Matthew 6:v7**..

Read

*..**[Romans 8]**..Read the entire chapter.. **[Matthew 10:v20]**.. For it is not ye that speak, but the spirit of your Father which speaks in you.. **[Matthew 6:v7]**..But when ye pray, use not vain repetitions , as the heathen do, for they think that they shall be heard for their much speaking..*

pp 128 /89 /262

I find to start the day on bended knees, head between legs, hands raised up a short yet straight to the point praising and pleading, quoting a corresponding bible verse or Psalm has never failed helping to get me through the toughest of days.. Its no co-incidence that there are exactly three separate bible verses speaking of this very holy act, and if done willingly will not have the other effect or better said; Bear the brunt of refusing to willingly (1) **Isaiah 45:v23** (2) **Romans 14:v11** (3) **Philippians 2:v10**..Ending the day in the same spirit opens the way for a good peaceful rest and sleep..

pg 92

pg 158 Read

*..**[Isaiah 45:v23]**..*
I have sworn by myself ,the word is gone out of my mouth in

Cross-reference

Read *righteousness, and shall not return, That unto me every knee shall bow, every tongue shall swear.. **[Romans 14:v11]**..For it is written, As I live saith the Lord, every knee shall bow to me, and every tongue shall confess to God..**[Philippians 2:v10/11]** .. That at the name of Jesus every knee should bow, of things in heaven and things in earth, and things under the earth. And that every tongue shall confess that Jesus Christ is Lord to the Glory of God the Father.*

pp 90/183

Three = perfection.

A word of warning !! Be careful of two types of utterances toward God or about God.. Many famous people including kings and commanders of armies, designers and builders have had their lives turned upside down by using the Lords name in vain or simply by making with Him promises or covenants.. **Judges 11:v30-40**.. the demise of the Titanic, John Lennon of the Beatles fame.. God will never not keep His covenant promise or agreement… Don't dare not to keep ours to Him..

Read *Read all verses..**[Judges 11:v30-40]**..And learn about God and Jeph'thah keeping to their vow.*

Last.. Unless Jesus Christ stops you in your tracks like he did with Saul who later became apostle Paul, or the word of God comes upon you, I know of NO other way of starting a relationship with God than by sincere heart rendered prayer.

NOTES

REALITY *of* ***REALITY***

MOVEMENT NUMBER 13

Host's

It's up to the individual to recognise the Lord's Host's. He is here.

Cross-reference

HOST'S

Hosts are a culmination of: weapons or armies God uses to remove or destroy His enemies to preserve and save His people, God cannot be defeated, these can be assumed to be weapons of war, they are Holy and have been manifested for this purpose often long before they are literally used, I will use an example from our original King James Bible to paint a real picture.. **1 Samuel 17:v45**..

Read

..[**1 Samuel 17:v45**]..Then said David to the Philistine, Thou comest to me with a sword, and with a spear, and with a shield: but I come to thee in the name of the Lord of Host's, the God of the armies of Israel, whom thou hast defied.

This Philistine was a Goliath a giant of a man, he tempted the Lord by calling out the army of the Israelites, Gods own people to harm them, to make them the slaves of his Philistine people, but because David had experiences of faith , yet a small young man, pulled the many host's together that the God had manifested for this holy battle, the outcome would be inevitable, the giant Goliath would be defeated, his head chopped off. Lets gather the type of Host's David knew he could count on. David had faith in his God; when he was just a shepherd boy tending his fathers flocks had delivered lambs from the jaws of a Lion and a Bear with his slingshot at the same time smote the predators, faith is a Host; this indeed happened prior to his confrontation with goliath..**1 Samuel 17:v35**..

Cross-reference

Read *And I went out after him, and smote him, and delivered it out of his mouth: and when he arose against me, I caught him by his beard and slew him..**[1 Samuel 17:v35]..***

And so when going into battle for the Lord, He is there and will have the final say on the outcome.. here are some of the Lords Host's in this David and Goliath battle: God had been predestined David to be King over Judah the northern kingdom long before this battle, having prepared him with lesser battles against the bear and lion, as mentioned and so anointing and serving God count as Hosts.. .. **1 Samuel 16:v1**.. His trust in God, love for the sheep, slingshot, stones, his shepherd's bag.. Davids pure heart..**1 Samuel 16:v7**..Are some of the visible and invisible Lord of host's, an army that can never be defeated..**1 Samuel 17:v40**.. and all prepared by and placed in its position of availability by the Lord.. more of the Lord of Host's that will always be in close proximity to the action, these are: angels, often not seen. The Holy spirit, His servant, in this instance the Prophet Samuel.

Read *..**[1 Samuel 16:1]** ..And the Lord said unto Samuel, How long will thou mourn for Saul, seeing I have rejected him from reigning over Israel ? fill thine horn with oil, and go, I will send thee to Jesse the Beth-lehmite: for I have provided Me a king among Jesse sons.. **[1Samuel 16:v7]**.. But the Lord said unto Samuel, look not at his countenance, or on the height of his stature; because I have refused him: for the Lord sees not as man sees; for man looks on the outward appearance, but the Lord looks on the heart*

Cross-reference

Read

*the heart..[**1 Samuel 17:v40**]..And he took his staff in his hand, and chose him five smooth stones out of the brook, and put them in a shepherd's bag which he had, even in a scrip; and his sling was in his hand: and he drew near to the Philistine.*

It can be and often is; that the Lord of Host's are either completely not recognized or rejected, sometimes difficulties to loss are allowed so that the Lord's help will be called upon and welcomed, yet very often, its other gods that are put in front of the all powerful God, in so like manner He moves aside or removes Himself completely from that person, or persons as was the cases in these events made mention..**1 Samuel 16:v14..1 Samuel Chapter 31**..

pg 215

Read

*..[**1 Samuel 16:v14**]..But the spirit of the Lord departed from Saul, and an evil spirit from the Lord troubled him..[**1 Samuel Chapter 31**].. Read the chapter.*

These host's are gathered together over time, but since the appearance of the Lord Jesus, these host's are no longer physical weaponry.. **John 18 :v11**.. Yet faith in the Gospel word used with love and truth.. **Ephesians 6:v11-20**..We will do well to know our accumulated host's of the Lord given through trials and tests spiritual battles: they might be patience, tolerance, steadfastness, humbleness of course.. Truth, righteousness, faith, the word and so on these are spiritual Host's, Jesus repaid no evil with evil..**1 Peter 3:v9**..For some this may seem impossible to accomplish, even wrong, and does not make human sense, a sure sign of weakness many may think, yet with each

Cross-reference

experience a strengthening to resist the temptations of evil is slowly developing albeit unseen, just as it did with David the little shepherd boy in the old testament, all in preparation to fight and defeat the giant Goliath and onto become the King of Israel.. how natural metamorphosis takes place in human kind just as it does with certain insects, butterfly's and creatures, how it shows us that.. God does not change. So where do we start, when do these hosts begin to reveal themselves in our lives ?, first !! not every person will pass through this journey, or path.

Read

*..[**John 18:v11**]..Then said Jesus unto Peter. Put up thy sword into the sheath: the cup which my Father hath given me, shall I not drink it ?..[**Ephesians 6:v11-18**].. Put on the whole armor of God, that ye may be able to stand against the wiles of the devil. For we wrestle not against principalities, against powers,against the rulers of the darkness of this world, against spiritual wickedness in high places. Wherefore take unto you the whole armor of God, that ye may be able to withstand in the evil day, and having done all, to stand. Stand therefore, having your loins girt about with truth, and having the breastplate of righteousness; And your feet shod with the preparation of the gospel of peace; Above all, taking the shield of faith, wherewith ye shall be able to quench all the fiery darts of the wicked. And take the helmet of salvation, and the sword of the Spirit, which is the word of God: Praying always with all prayer and supplication in the Spirit, and watching thereunto with all perseverance and supplication for all the saints.*

pp 55/144

Cross-reference

pg 246

Read *..[**1Peter 3:v9**]..Not rendering evil for evil or railing for railing, but contrariwise blessing blessing; knowing that you are thereunto called, that you should inherit a blessing.*

Spiritual Host's amount or add up through the experiences of faith made when applying the word of the Gospel of Jesus Christ to defeat the evil one, faith is in the word, the word becomes a weapon against the forces of evil and darkness.
Satan the tempter is out to draw people away from following Jesus Christ to destroy, Jesus and the Holy Spirit are out to lead people to himself to total salvation and everlasting freedom.
Jesus is more powerful than Satan, Jesus is everywhere all at the same time, his Gospel will expose the works of darkness (lies/deceit) because it is light (truth) ..**James 4:v7**.. it is necessary to have spiritual battles in which faith in the Almighty God through Jesus the word that many small victories can be gained, these small victories will provide the greater perseverance and persistence needed to quench the fiery darts of the wicked one, that will not stop until the Lord says so, and you are strong enough in faith, **Ephesians 6:v16.** to be for His use in the future tasks that are inevitable, these will be in the thousand year

RR kingdom of peace, to be spoken about in ***Reality of Reality*** book **2**..

Read *Submit yourselves therefore to God Resist the devil and he will flee from you..[**James 4:v7**]..*

Obstacles must either be removed or a way made to go round them, either way Gods will, will be done, nothing can stand in His way of achieving this will, God does not need anyone to accomplish what He pleases, however He desires all flesh to come to know Him and so offers

Cross-reference

this great opportunity through battles with the wicked one, He has already resisted all the temptations of the devil..

Matthew Chapter 4 ..Uttering the words and admonition, I come in the name of the Lord of Host's is a conviction that Jesus Christ is with, yet the enemy wants to do battle, having gathered many spiritual experiences through faith, the outcome is that the devil will flee, the

RR ***Reality of Reality*** is this: the Lord of Hosts is here, its up to the individual to recognize Him and call on the Lord for the purpose to defeat the enemy.. the wicked one

pp 48 /52 of all.. the devil.

..[**Matthew Chapter 4:v 1-11**]..Read all the **verses** in your **OKJB**.

NOTES

REALITY *of* ***REALITY***

MOVEMENT NUMBER 14

Kings, Queens, Princes, Princesses

Royal Status in this life does not guarantee the same in the next life, yet could be the opposite.

Cross-reference

KINGS, QUEENS, PRINCES, PRINCESSES

There has to be high ranked persons in our world to reign, leaders, governors, exalted ones, chiefs, captains, Lords etc and the King as mentioned, why ? thats how it is in God's kingdom, God is the King and the King appoints others to serve Him only, yet there is no mention of God the king having a queen, that's why God is really the only King of Kings and Lord of Lords..

..Revelation 19:v16..

He is Sovereign and that's that.

pg 244 Read

..[Revelation 19:v16]...*And he hath on his vesture and on his thigh a name written;*

KING OF KINGS, AND LORD OF LORDS..

God through Jesus Christ shows the world's Kings how they are to rule over their Kingdom, Kings don't reign they rule, a king has the power and authority to rule over his kingdom how he wishes, he can be totally ruthless and go so far as to see himself as a God figure, one whom must be worshiped in whichever way he commands, a king like this will answer to the king of kings, because God the king will be the judge over all kings that ever ruled on the earth, in the reality of things the kings of the earth are placed onto their thrones by the king of kings from His throne in His Kingdom, and that true everlasting king will surely expect the world's kings to rule over their kingdoms in honor of the **KING OF KINGS,** for they have not placed themselves in the seat of a king, even if a king has over-thrown a neighboring king, that king could not have, if God had not willed the outcome that way.. **Daniel 2:v21**..

Cross-reference

Read *And He changes the times and the seasons,: He removes kings, and sets up kings: He giveth wisdom unto the wise, and knowledge to them that know understanding..[**Daniel 2:v21**]..*

God allows the earthly kings to have great power, wealth and authority even to have a royal queen to reign with him, this reign is powerless without the king,in other words, a queen that has no king is subject to other authorities, governors parliaments or senates, therefore her reign is subject to the laws and conditions imposed upon her, which could put her out of favor with God should these cause her to disobey any of the ten commandments, the ***Reality of***
RR ***Reality*** in this movement is; status in this life does not guarantee nor lead to a similar Royal status in the next life, yet could be the opposite. Coming back to a king, no amount of power wealth or achievements will cause a favored entry into the next life, but how his rule resembled that of how God rules fulfilled by the physical appearance of Jesus Christ around 2020 years ago for Jesus fulfilled the law and the prophets.. **Matthew 5:v17**..Jesus life on earth is true to the very life of God his father in His kingdom of heaven, Jesus is a king but not an earthly king, earthly kings store up earthly riches to gain control through power and might over his people, often oppressing them through taxation and one sided laws and rules, disregarding the laws, commands of God not to covet, or over tax.

Jesus Christ is not that type of king, Jesus is the king to his people through giving, sharing, freeing, suffering for his own through a life of serving, being the least,

Cross-reference

to the extent of being persecuted and then crucified, yet not before leaving a trail of evidence that one day will be used by His Father the Almighty God and judge at judgment day.. Jesus life as the king of the Jews.. his people or subjects would be served by him first, he was to pay with his life for their debts of sin and not impose punishment a contrast to the many kings that have come and gone out of the world's nations.. **Matthew 2:v2**..

Read

*..**[Matthew 2:v2]**..Saying where is he that is born king of the Jews ? For we have seen his star in the east, and are come to worship him.. **[Matthew 5:v17]**..Think not that I am come to destroy the law, or the prophets: I am not come to destroy but fulfill.*

pp 130 /143 /214 /29

During the period of the kings as recorded in the Old Testament bible, out of **42** kings, **36** did evil in the sight of God, these evil kings met with sorrowful pitiful deaths, their rights as king had not accompanied them into the realm of the dead, what could have been for them a different

RR

Reality of Reality than the one already mentioned was not to be and what should have boar a warning to kings following on from other kings either through lineage or military standing or other, did not and no matter any achievements brought during the rule and reign of these **36 King's,** they counted for nothing in the sight of God who looks on the heart, kings and queens, royalty are just as much accountable for their life works, as any ordinary walk about the streets person.

Cross-reference

So what makes for an evil king.. **1 Kings 16:v25**.. and **v30** the age old evil that God cannot tolerate, erecting a temple and statues of other so called god's, raising up a son to take up the throne to continue a family legacy of opposing the one and only real living God whom sat these kings upon their thrones, these godless rulings would come to end either through painful defeat in conflict or sudden death.
..**1Kings18;16-40**..
A God fearing queen as was Esther will look out for the wellbeing of her King and subjects.. with courage, she saved her people from genocide..

Read

Esther 5/6.. that God could accept. prince' and princesses fall under the same banner.
..[1 Kings 16:v25].. *But Omri wrought evil in the eyes of the Lord, and did worse than all that were before him..[**v30**] .. And Ahab the son of Omri did evil in the sight of the Lord , above all that were before him..* ***[1 Kings 18:16-40] ..***

Read

Read all verses; consider you kings and queens of the world today, you royalty and everyone every where that God accepts NO ONE putting idols or other kinds of worshiping before **Him.**
GOD MUST BE FIRST THROUGH JESUS CHRIST.

NOTES

REALITY *of* ***REALITY***

MOVEMENT NUMBER 15

The Number Three

The number three is perfection in God or in the devil.

Cross-reference

THE NUMBER THREE

Numbers have been significantly implanted into God's nature as have been seed sowing, reaping.. three things coming together as ONE.. three defines perfection, three is the creator of everything that is.. Was.. and will ever be.. The Almighty Lord: The GODHEAD.. **Colossians 2:v9-10.. Acts 17:v29** Father, Son, Holy Ghost three components, joined as ONE. the Triune God. The number three or three components is found in nature, three is the strongest formation that exists, stemming out of the creator, what gives the strength, the power is when all three are in oneness, three pieces of rope strained together are stronger than individually strained.

Read ..***[Colossians 2:v9-10]***..*For in him dwells all the fullness of the Godhead bodily And ye are complete in him, which is the head of all principality and power.*

Read ..***[Acts 17:v29]***.. *For as much then as we are the offspring of God, we ought not to think that the Godhead is like unto gold, or silver, or stone, graven by art and man's device.*

The strength, or the power, or the righteousness lie in all the three components being joined into one; having the same goal, purpose, desire, bearing the same witness, to do right, to be in all truth,This is a long list which is determined by the required outcome, which is determined by the one being served, God or the devil.

WE WOULD LOOK AT SERVING GOD FIRST. Always we look to Jesus as our example, he represents the Godhead on earth, Jesus is totally

Cross-reference

one with God his father and the holy Ghost, the truth is all three agree as one and bear record as one in heaven and in earth..**1 John 5v7 and v8**..

Read

*For there are three that bear record in heaven,the Father, the word, and the Holy Ghost: and these three are one. And there are three that bear witness in earth, the spirit, and the water, and the blood: and these three agree as one.,..**[1 John 5:v7-8]**..*

pp 198 /58

Jesus of course is the word, the water is baptism, the blood is his body.. three components that are witness to God visiting earth and mankind in Jesus Christ, to sacrifice his life in exchange for our sins, this confirms the outcome in mind was for the saving of mankind and how three components binding as one are become a powerful determined unstoppable force. Here are some other three things coming together as one.. man, woman and God joined together to form a union in marriage. Man, woman and God to produce children. Sand, cement and water to produce concrete. Three sides joined together to form a strong structure, especially in the building and construction industry. From the 4 examples above, the first two with God: when Godly things are done with the presence of God, they are done right and attract His favor or blessing God is the creator of marriage, He has commanded that man and woman are first married before engaging in sexual activities, they should keep their virgin until marriage and so bearing children is the result after marriage..**1 Corinthians 7:v36/37** should the married couple desire and so the three become

Cross-reference

one in God, in marriage; the couple, husband and wife become one flesh in marriage.. **Genesis 2:v23-25**..

Read

*..[**1 Corinthians** 7:v36-37].. But if any man think that he behaves himself uncomely toward his virgin, if she pass the flower of her age, and need so require, let him do what he will, he sins not: let them marry. Nevertheless he that stands steadfast in his heart, having no necessity, but hath power over his own will, and hath so decreed in his heart that he will keep his virgin, does well. ..[**Genesis 2:v23-25**]..And Adam said, This is now bone of my bones, and flesh of my flesh: she shall be called Woman, because she was taken out of Man. There fore shall a man leave his father and his mother, and shall cleave unto his wife: and they shall be one flesh. And they were both naked, the man and his wife, and were not ashamed.*

Marriage becomes a relevant example of the number three when God is the third part. The other two examples have been passed onto mankind by God through his omniscience or all knowing, what the cement will be used for will become the third part or the motive.. Examples: a wall for protection or division, to build a house for family, a church for the honor and glory of God, a prison to separate criminals from society. Now!! there is one other number three that is to be one, the most serious and it is directly related to you and me, people everywhere and that is our person our body, soul and spirit..**1 Thessalonians 5:v23**..And they

Cross-reference

too need to agree as one what we think must be the same as what we say and do.. Of course to the honor and Glory of God.

Read

pg 59

*..[**1 Thessalonians 5:v23**].. And the very God of peace sanctify you wholly; and I pray God your whole spirit and soul and body be preserved blameless unto the coming of our Lord Jesus Christ.*

So far above all the examples above are inclusive of God being the number three in the equation, the third part or the motive and reason behind one and two coming together if there is any misalignment in other word: thinking one thing then saying or doing something else, will be a total misalignment, confusion will set in and at the end of the life, after many years functioning this way, the end result will be disorientation, a condition I consider to be the worst life work, not having lived a life where clear cut decisions and choices were thought, said and done. This happens when God or the Godhead in Jesus Christ is not the focus, instead the devil is, the motive is neither in obeying the God given commandments, nor for the wellbeing of the other part the other person, neither a single person if there is no other person in the equation,whichever way it goes three is perfected in the one being served. Some more typical examples of serving the devil where he becomes the third part having a sexual relationship without the bond of a marriage between the man and woman.. having children out of wedlock.. And so anywhere perfection is the end result the number three is linked either in whole

Cross-reference

or in division.. In whole : Jonah spent three days and three nights in the belly of the big fish.. **Jonah 1:v17**.. Jesus after he was crucified spent the same three days in the depths of hell to preach to the souls whom once disobeyed God..

Matthew12:v 40.. Some final examples.. all of these are divisible by **3**: **12** months which is a year.. **42** months which is the duration of a human pregnancy..**144000** which are the number of the redeemed from the earth.. **Revelation 14:v1**..
The **12** tribes of Israel..

Read *..**[Jonah 1:v17]**..Now the Lord had prepared a great fish to swallow up Jonah. And Jonah was in the belly of the fish three days and three*
pg 195 *nights. ..**[Matthew 12:v40]**..For as Jonah was three days and three nights in the whales's belly: so shall the son of man be three days and three*
pg 250 *nights in the heart of the earth..**[Revelation 14:v1]**..ANDI looked, and, lo ,a Lamb stood on the mount Zion, and with him an **hundred forty** and **four thousand**, having his Fathers's name written in their foreheads.*

NOTE !! When God has predestined, three or a higher number equally divisible by it, HE is in close proximity.

MOVEMENT NUMBER 16

Idolatry

Idolatry in any form is temporary gain with eternal consequences.

Cross-reference

IDOL WORSHIP

This is sinful practice rated up with any of the early sins as an evil that the Almighty God will not let go unpunished, He must be worshiped and only Him, God will re-visit those doing this and judge righteously..
..**Leviticus 19:v4** and **Leviticus 26:v21..**

Read .. ***[Leviticus 19:v4]..*** *Turn you not unto idols, nor make to yourselves molten gods. I am the Lord your God.*

Read .. ***[Leviticus 26:v21]..*** *And if you walk contrary unto Me, and will not hearken unto Me; I will bring seven times more plagues upon you according to your sins..*

Idol worship is so rife today in the 21st century especially among teenagers and even more so with teenage girls, sorrow and sadness like never before will be the order of this day and age.
So what what is idolatry and what is its attraction??
Two question marks virtually inseparable, the attraction is to redirect focus.. towards any other thing, object or person, other than God and Jesus Christ..
RR actually the ***Reality of Reality***.. is truth.
This can be a pop star, group, the self, Its my life I can do with it what I please, enjoy myself make the most of it, live my life to the fullest, after all I am not harming anyone according to the self.
There is so much on offer today to focus on, to spend most of the time indulging in, that the commands and laws of God just don't feature, the very essence of life Jesus Christ is life and life eternal, that no other thing, person or power can give except Christ.. **Mark 16:v16..**
A life focused on any other name, his gospel's will most assuredly lead to a

Cross-reference

RR distanced life from the ***Reality of Reality*** of why this very existence is, life is created for God's purpose or cause and that is to get to know Him, to learn His ways, to obey and worship Him alone for He is a jealous God.. **Exodus 20:v3** to.. **v5**

Read *He that believes and is baptized, shall be saved; but he that believes not shall be damned..* ***[Mark 16:v16]..***

pp 145 /85
pg 254

Read ***[Exodus 20:v3-5]***..*Thou shalt have no other Gods before me. Thou shalt not make unto thee any graven image, or any likeness of any thing that is in heaven above, or that is in the earth beneath, or that is in the water under the earth. Thou shalt not bow down thyself to them, nor serve them: for I am the Lord thy God am a jealous God, visiting the iniquity of the fathers upon the children unto the third and fourth generation of them that hate me.*

When one turns their focus away from Jesus Christ which is God to any other and willing to do anything / give up all to find favor with that idol no matter what the idol or idols are (listed above are some) the will of God, his commands and statutes wont be even considered and this lifestyle if not realized and turned away from can end very abruptly crushingly, leaving other family members and friends blaming God, yet He would have tried more than once to reveal things were not right.. perhaps through a not so happy conscience.. **Romans 2:v13-16**.. God has given us this gift to let us know that He is a Jealous God as told in the **Read** the bible chapters and verses portion, this jealousy over His chosen people can lead to an

Cross-reference

act of God out of how He feels, yet no matter what happens, God will always act righteously, He cannot be held into question for anything.

Read

..***[Romans 2:v13-16]***..*(For not the hearers of the law are just before God, but the doers of the law shall be justified. For when the Gentiles, which have not the law, do by nature the things contained in the law, these, having not the law, are a law unto themselves: Which shew the work of the law written in their hearts, their conscience also bearing witness, and their thoughts, the mean while accusing or else excusing one another).*

Focusing on anyone or anything other than the Almighty God, His commandments and laws, His son Jesus the word [gospels] through a life beset in the worldly for the flesh can lead away from the spiritual, some of which are made mentioned here.. for God is spirit. Spirit is life, all graven or molten physical things, though it or they might resemble a real person having features like a human, a head, a body, limbs etc, yet made out of materials, stone, iron, even if made out of exotics, bronze, gold or something these things have no life and can offer nothing, the hands that sculpted these things can not put life in them, not even if these things are robotic.

RR

The ***Reality of Reality*** is this: Idolatry of this kind is beset in the mind, to make idols of any of these, will lead to nothing, the physical things made by man, are born out of the mind of man trying to imitate the creator, man is made by the creator God, not the other way round.
All life which is spiritual is from God.
..Exodus 32:v7-8.. Habakkuk 2:v18

Cross-reference

Molten image: a poured out liquid to form an object or figure, often made out of precious substance like gold or bronze, yet lifeless as mentioned with the Graven the

RR The ***Reality of Reality*** is first beset in the mind..

Daniel 3 people: the flesh..
Especially among teenagers this form of idolatry knows no limitations or boundaries, it is not out of the question that the desires to be rich and famous amidst society.. for instance; pop stars, actors, models, business people, can bring financial stability and security, power to pull strings, call the shots, yet all these types of benefits have one thing in common, they are all temporary and not life sustaining, man has no power over life and death..
Daniel 3.

Money: To worship and adore this particular idol, is the root of all evil, hardly an idol is worshiped without the worshiper expecting to be enriched with money and goods, also not life sustaining, meaning temporal, just for the flesh life..**1 Timothy 6:v10.**.

Read ***Matthew 27:3-5**.. and all **Daniel chapter 3..** from your **OKJB.***
BE especially focused on the reward bestowed on Daniels three friends. Shadrach, Meshach, and Abednego.. be mindful of their obedience and trust in the only true living God without which no one will receive His promises of eternal life and from the fire of eternal damnation.. **Matthew 25:v41**.. Reserved for those whom don't trust and worship the Almighty Lord God only.

Cross-reference

Read

*..**[Matthew25:v41]**..Then shall he say also unto hem on the left hand.*
Depart from eye cursed, into everlasting fire prepared for the devil and his angels. without which no one will receive His promises of eternal life and from the fire of eternal damnation. Reserved for those whom don't trust and worship the Almighty Lord God

Read

*.. **[Exodus 32:v7-8]**.. And the Lord said: Go get thee down; for thy people, which you have brought out of the land of Egypt, have corrupted themselves. ..**[1 Timothy 6:v10]**.. For the love of money is the root of all evil: which while some coveted after, they have erred from the faith and pierced themselves through with many sorrows.*

pp 163 /238

*..**[Habakkuk 2:v18]**.. What profits the graven image that the maker thereof hath graven it; the molten image, and a teacher of lies, that the maker of his work trusts therein, to make dumb idols?*

REALITY *of* ***REALITY***

MOVEMENT NUMBER 17

Respect and Respecter

Favouritism or partiality in any manner will not bring the same with God.

Cross-reference

RESPECT AND RESPECTER

I hear often people say.. I respect him or her, but ?, I respect their opinion, but? I respect this , but ? I respect that , but ? Just how many respects are there ? this is my question by the way. So is there somethings wrong here ? If so what is it ? The first task or thing to do after making mention of this: God is no respecter of persons.. **Acts 10: v34** is to establish the real meaning of respect.

Read *..Then Peter opened his mouth, and said, Of a truth I perceive that God is no respecter of persons..[**Acts 10:v34**]..*

pg 210 According to dictionary: A feeling of deep admiration for someone or some thing elicited by their abilities, qualities or achievements.. this would suggest that a respecter of persons will depend on what a person does, either for them directly, or just what they see is good or right by their own measurement, put another way this type of relationship is dependent or based on work done,in this a definite ulterior motive exists. A motive as this would suggest that God is not found in this type of relationship, God is no respecter of persons and so cannot be part of this kind of relationship because it is sin to treat people different to how we ourselves would want to be treated..**James2:v9**..

And could be considered as partiality..

James 3:v17..Its this type of behavior that God cannot be part of or associated with for His treatments are the same towards everyone according to his righteousness.

Cross-reference

pg 284

Read *..[James 2:v9]..But if ye have respect to persons, ye commit sin, and are convinced of the law as transgressors.. [James 3:v17]..But the wisdom that is from above is first pure, then peaceable, gentle, and easy to be entreated, full of mercy and good fruits, without partiality, and without hypocrisy.*

Always we look to God through the life of Jesus Christ and His gospel this includes the old testament, I will make understanding why a relationship derived out of such behavior is fixed in what it is;When God is the focus, the focus is: I am doing or just agreeing with what is said and or done for no benefit of my own, there can be no respecter in this kind of relationship and God will be happy, this no respect is first towards ourselves, for no personal gain or benefit.. God out of the love and truth for His creation is able to bestow any reward due by of his nature and character, which we know as a blessing.. **Hebrews 6:v14**..

Read *Saying.. Surely blessing I will bless thee, and multiplying, I will multiply thee..*
[Hebrews 6:v14]..

The world in which we live is driven by favoritism, those in high places will first see to their counterparts or those whom join allegiance with for this purpose, not so much as seeking the same with the Almighty God, this is a fatal mistake and can only lead to a judicable notion, this type clearly came to light in way the richer nations zapped up huge Covid -19 vaccines ahead of the poorer nations and the way in which these vaccines were rolled out or administered and

Cross-reference

required.

A lifestyle that grows dependent on this method to attain relationships allies or success for the individual even a nation can expect it this way, the fight or battle will not have the support or backing of God, His angels or hosts,

RR leading to a ***Reality of Reality*** defeat from all sides and areas in simple words, nothing gained, moving into and out of relationships, where partiality or favoritism is the building block or cornerstone will not be hidden by persons whom do not... **James 2: v1-6**..

Read *..[**James 2:v1-6**]..My brethren, have not the faith of our Lord Jesus Chris, the Lord of glory, with respect of person. For if there come unto your assembly a man with a gold ring, in goodly apparel, and there come in also a poor man in vile raiment; And ye have respect to him that wears the gay clothing, and say unto him, sit thou here in a good place; and say to the poor, stand thou there, or sit here under my footstool: are ye not then partial in yourselves, and are become judges of evil thoughts ? Hearken my beloved brethren,Hath not God chosen the poor of this world rich in faith, and heirs of the Kingdom, which He hath promised to them that love Him ? But ye have despised the poor. Do not rich men oppress you, and draw you before the judgment seats ?*

The **BUT**.. Mentioned in our opening sentence, I respect you, **BUT** what is this for ? In the context of the same as written above, which is respecting for the self, I respect you because I want for myself even if its just recognition adding this thing, BUT.. I am going to lower myself to you,

Cross-reference

to your expertise yet keep in reserve something in the equation for myself, something that I can or have done to put me up there above you as the one that deserves praise, the reward. Lets establish what the true meaning of respect and respecter in the sight of the Lord our God through Jesus Christ is.

God looks at each deed or doing for its true **face value**, it does not matter who is doing the saying or the doing, or what is being said or done, yet for the benefit of whom?Whom is being the honored.

To finish of there are two examples that go right back to the early stages of man where God utters these first His first respect word; saying I respect not.. **Genesis 4;v4**.. I have not respect.. **Genesis 4: v5**.. **ANSWER :**

Read

..*[**Genesis 4:v3-7**].. And in process of time it came to pass, that Cain brought of the fruit of the ground an offering unto the Lord. And Abel, he also brought of the first-lings of his flock and of the fat thereof. And the Lord had respect unto Abel and to his offering: But unto Cain and his offering he had not respect, And Cain was very wroth, and his countenance fell. And the Lord said unto Cain, Why art thou wroth ? And why is thy countenance fallen ? If thou doest well, shalt thou not be accepted ? And if thou doest not well, sin lies at the door. And unto thee shall be his desire, and thou shalt rule over him.*

God is no respecter right from the start, He does not force anyone how to live, their life, yet the outcome or reward or wages will be the result of choice, that choice is to obey and please God or other..

Cross-reference

One last example how Jesus treats everyone with the same measure is to be found in the Gospel of **Matthew 20:v1-16**

Read

pg 91

*Jesus offers workers the same pay, one penny before they begin work yet he hires them at different times of the day and pays all; the same one Penny, this causes some to question, yet Jesus merely points out that what belongs to him , he can do with as he pleases, this is a reference to those who labor in his work, the amount of time or the amount of work done does not persuade his Father to look any more favorable on the one over the other because of what they did...**[Matthew 20:v1-16}..***

MOVEMENT NUMBER 18

Will of God

God is willing to save from eternal death, yet not willing to by force.

Cross-reference

WILL OF GOD

The scriptures are filled with the mentioning of the will of God, a good example is the Lords prayer, the prayer the Lord taught us.. **Matthew 6:v9**.. In it: Thy will be done in earth, as it is in heaven.

Read

[Matthew 6:v9].. *Our Father which art in heaven, Hallowed be thy name. Thy kingdom come. Thy will be done in earth, as it is in heaven. Give us this day our daily bread. And forgive us our debts, as we forgive our debtors. And lead us not into temptation, but deliver us from evil: For thine is the kingdom, and the power and the glory, for ever Amen.*

pp 89 /92 /262

This will of God notion or idea that everything happens at the will of God, oh!! It was God's will that's why it happened that way, often used to justify wrong or non productive actions, world wars happened because it was the will 0f God.

It is as if the world is blaming the creator God and saying that he is happy to see people that He lovingly created blown to pieces, killed or maimed, leaving families broken, dispersed, widows and orphans, this is just so far from the truth that the all loving faithful God and scene of any day.

When examining the will of God in the moment we must apply some fixtures.. God can not be tempted to do evil.. **James 1:v13.**. God will not do evil or wickedly.. **Job 34:v12..** He makes known the end from the beginning.

Isaiah 46:v10.. meaning God has all the time to set things into His will according to the plans, that He has for the future does not rely on anyone, time, a single moment or event to achieve his desired will for the final outcome

Cross-reference

can pass, yet at the right time and moment, the place, be assured His will be the final will to be done, just as He saw it way back in the beginning, because is to save all men, yet not willing to force,
RR this is the ***Reality of Reality.***

Read *.**[James 1:v13]**.. Let no man say when he is tempted, I am tempted of God: for God cannot be tempted with evil, neither He tempts any man.. **[Job 34:v12]..** You surely God will not do wickedly, neither will the Almighty per vent judgment..**[Isaiah 46;v10]**.. Declaring the end from the beginning, and from ancient times the things that are not yet done saying, My counsel shall stand, and I will do all my pleasure.*

The will of God cannot be influenced yet because of His desire to have a right relationship with and rescue all of mankind from their sinful nature and because He knows everything even our thoughts, which is an open book to Him, He is willing to make His powerful influence of nature available to the pure in heart that wrestle with Him for the right reason and outcome, some examples:
Read **Genesis 32:v22-32**..**Genesis 16:v16-33.**. God made this known when He gave Moses the Ten commandments on Mt SINAI, these commands were already being transgressed, God stepped in at this time as an Act of His love, He had given mankind the freedom to choose how to behave and treat one another as neighbors, how to acknowledge Him, their Almighty creator, yet how some was behaving and especially the rulers of the day not pleasing to His nature and will, and so to help He issued in a set of Ten good markers in these commands, bridging an unknown specified gap so to speak, and there would be No not knowing the will of God from that moment, and God would send His son

Cross-reference

Jesus Christ some thousands of years later to fulfill all those laws and commandments as was pronounced by the prophets long before.. **Matthew 5:v17-20..** fulfilling another Act of love and grace on mankind that He had previously announced back in the garden of Eden to the serpent and tempter to sin that He would deal with Him (Devil) .. **Genesis3:v5..**

pp 143 /100 /214 /291

Read ***.[Matthew 5:v17-20].*** *Think not that I am come to destroy the the law, or the prophets I am not come to destroy, but to fulfill. For very I say unto you, Till heaven and earth pass, not one jot or one tittle shall in no wise pass from the law, till all be fulfilled. Whosoever therefore shall break one of these least commandments, and shall teach men to do so, he shall be called the least in the kingdom of heaven: For I say unto you, That except your righteousness shall exceed the righteousness of the Scribes and Pharisees, you shall in no case enter the kingdom of heaven. .* ***[Genesis 3:v15]***..*And I will put enmity between thy seed and her seed; and it shall bruise thy head,and you shall bruise his heel.*

pg 142

Read **(Try to do this thing)**.. *Align the right OKJB verses to your whole life as they come your way to action, your mind and thoughts, feelings, emotions, when choosing and deciding.*

Read *...from your* ***OKJB .. [Genesis 32:v22-32] and [Genesis 16:v16-33}..***

Through Jesus Christ came the fullness of God the Father in a person of the flesh and blood, the word [God] the word was incarnate, a physical form that would be seen and heard, and could also be touched.

Cross-reference

God the Almighty creator of heaven and earth, the visible and invisible creation is alive in the physical figure, Jesus Christ, not only does Jesus speak the words, these words are the spiritual God, the creator of the physical creation, Jesus also put the same action to the words, this culminated in the event of the cross, that has fulfilled the expression, a lamb led to the slaughter, this is the will of God, Jesus is the will of God.. **Isaiah 53:v7..**

pg 286

Read ***..[Isaiah 53:7]..****He was oppressed , and he was afflicted, yet he opened not his mouth: he is brought as a lamb to the slaughter, and as a sheep before her shearers is dumb, so he opened not his mouth.*

All followers [disciples] of Jesus in the same word will live and proclaim the same, then by the will and power of Himself, God would see to it that his brought to life word, would not just remain preserved just in a story, it was to spread around the world to action in the form of the book known as the Holy King James Bible, and out of it, to preserve that WILL, in His presence after the crucifixion of His son Jesus Christ in the forming of His one Holy spiritual church..
..Matthew 16:v18.. [always the two]. it is in this church [members in a joined body] ordinary persons would continue to live in and through its followers, transforming many different members into this one body believing in Christ and the cross..**1 Corinthians 12:v12..** as many as will come believe and be joined.
This is the will of God to save all flesh.. not to do harm or kill, but to save.. **1 Timothy 2:v4..** for God takes NO pleasure in watching the wicked suffer and die, but it would be by His will, that they should repent and change..
..Ezekiel 18:v32..

Cross-reference

Read *And I say also unto thee, That thou art Peter, and upon this rock I will build my church; and the gates of hell shall not prevail against it..* ***[Matthew16:v18]***

pp 175 /182 /220 /36

Read ***[1Corinthians 12:v12]****.. For as the body is one, and hath many members, and all the members of that one body, being many, are one body: so also is Christ.*

pg 182

Read *..****[1 Timothy 2:v4]****.. Who will have all men to be saved, and to come unto the knowledge of the truth..*

Read ***..[Ezekiel 18:v32]..****For I have no pleasure in the death of him that dies, says the Lord God: Wherefore turn yourselves and live you.*

REALITY *of* ***REALITY***

MOVEMENT NUMBER 19

Diseases in Diverse Places

Man will not turn off the supply to his own diseases.

Cross-reference

DISEASES IN DIVERSE PLACES

The world in general know what diseases are, what these mostly unseen things can do, how they ravage the physical body from inside out, the pain caused by these viruses, oft times without any real warning or sometimes ignored by the host these are real things, living organisms, they don't: fear, respect, feel, listen have emotions, sympathize, listen, obey or answer to anyone, subject to law, quantity, time, they are who they are, cannot be influenced by teaching, they don't have a brain and so cant reason, so why are they here, keep multiplying just keep on coming, keep on diversifying showing up in the diverse of places, (various in character manifold) why have governments with all their power, might, monetary wealth, partners scientific advisers, professors, modern technology, inventive skills not been able to identify nor rid mankind of these diseases or find out where they come from, what actually causes them to specifically drive towards mankind? As always I am going to turn to the Holy Bible for answers.. **Matthew 4:v23-24**.. Prophecies diseases will come.. This has never been a secret, yet a mystery revealed long before our time, for our time, for times gone by, all times and periods. Pestilences these fall in the same category, they destroy they eat, they devour sometimes so veracious in their wake, often leaving utter desolation in the lands these plagues affect all life yet human life falls helpless under the brunt of its destructive powers, the same comments of facts apply to these types..

Matthew 24:v7.. Luke 21:v11..

pp 164 / 141 /71

Cross-reference

Read **[Matthew 4:v23-24]**.. and Jesus went about all Galilee, teaching in their synagogues, and preaching the gospel of the kingdom, and healing al manner of sickness and all manner of disease among the people.. v24 and his fame went throughout all Syria: and they brought unto him all sick people that were taken with divers diseases and torments, and those which were possessed with devils, and those that had the palsy; and he healed them. First!! to be recognized from the events mentioned in the bible chapters above, is that Jesus preached the Kingdom of God, in the kingdom there are none of these conditions mentioned, which means that by living in the kingdom of God now already, following the life and teaching of Jesus Christ in other words, these lesser sickness and diseases will either not come upon that person but if it did? Jesus is still here to work his healing miracles revealing His kingdom at the same time, for it is all about the Kingdom of God to Jesus Christ. Second !! Those possessed with devils and the palsy have usually been exposed too and welcomed them by inviting them in, these greater exposed torments or works of devils are also healed by Jesus, yet will come back with seven more spirits more wicked than first upon that person if welcomed back again... **Matthew 12 :v43-45**..

Read ***[Matthew 12 :v43-45]***..*When the unclean spirit is gone out of a man, he walks through dry places, seeking rest, and finds none. Then he saith, I will return into my house from whence I came out; and when he is come, he finds*

Cross-reference

Read

it empty swept, and garnished. Then goes he, and taketh with himself seven other spirits more wicked than himself, and they enter in and dwell there: and the last state of that man is worse than the first. Even so shall it be also unto this wicked generation.

These events are recorded in the time of Jesus Christ yet he prophesied they would come again.. **Matthew 24:v7-8**.. I will say they have not stopped, history writes that they haven't. Christ is saying watch out for these things happening in a big way because they are signs of my return.

Read

[**Matthew 24:v7**].. For nation shall rise against nation, and kingdom against kingdom: and there shall be famines, and pestilences and earthquakes, in divers places..v8 all these are the beginning of sorrows. Whether come diseases, pestilences, plagues, famines or earthquake, man is powerless to subdue them, for the plain reason that they are caused by man or through disobedience have brought them upon themselves, by turning away from God and his commands. The further mankind distances himself from the creator the greater the power and forces of nature will turn on him in a grand display of sowing and reaping. Divers places.. What does this mean? What is the significance? There are manifold and various not just numerically but many variants too, by number these divers places are wide spread across and through out the world and the human population, no matter the area or place where there is life, these destructors can show

Cross-reference

up and take up residency in their host, so many ways for this to happen, passed around in the air, by the blowing wind, transported from area to area by: people, the wild life, goods and services generated by man, through the exchanging of products from country to country, it is just not likely that these passages will be closed off because they are simply day to day events having been put in place to sustain this natural life.

RR

Reality of Reality is this: Because man has a propensity to sin, a persistent desire and need to live above God, be as a God, ignore God.. disobey Him that diseases in divers places can not be contained. Significance is the revelation to the prophesies in Gods word, having been told of centuries ago to come true years later should tell mankind, leaders in all sectors, that the words recorded in holy stricture are living words, these words not only speak but they also come alive, it's the same way with the various pestilences, earthquakes written words coming alive somewhere out in the midst of populated areas reeking havoc amongst the dwellers often leaving no escape route without the help or support of the outside. It is worth mentioning that some of the above were called out by God as a direct call for change of heart and attitude, we read

so.. **Exodus 7, 8, 9 and 10**.. Yet disobedience, the change of heart never completely went away, remaining to this day, so too are these consequences named and mentioned above..

Read

..**[Exodus chapters 7-10]**.. read out of your **OKJB.**

Cross-reference

In these four chapters of Exodus, God creates 10 plagues or pestilences to show He is Sovereign, His reign and rule is supreme. He confirms that even in diseases He is there ready to protect even rescue, nothing is too hard for Him, obeying His command certainly is reserved for His own people, meaning those that hear Him and do what He says will have a different outcome than those that do not.

REALITY *of* ***REALITY***

MOVEMENT NUMBER 20

Governments

All high power and governance is subject to the higher power GOD.

Cross-
reference

GOVERNMENTS

Mankind is subject to all the powers of nature, there is no escaping what God sets in its place, this natural includes Governments, world leaders and powers, God is a leader, a king, He rules the entire visible and invisible universe, God is the sovereign ruler and supreme power over everything that is was and is to come, there cannot be any other model for righteous rule than the Almighty nor can there be any other system, it has to be this way, because the Lord says so, He is the government whom institutes all governments, setting the standard for all governance.. **Psalms 22:v28.. Romans 13:v1-7**..

Read

*[**Proverbs 22:v28**]..For the kingdom is the LORD'S :and he is the governor among the nations..[**Romans 13:v1-7**]..Let every soul be subject unto the higher powers For there is no power but of God : the powers that be are ordained of God. Whosoever therefore resists the power, resists the ordinance of God: and they that resist shall receive to themselves damnation. For rulers are not a terror to good works, but to the evil, Wilt thou then not be afraid of the power? Do that which is good, and thou shalt have praise of the same. For he is the minister of God to thee for good, But if thou do that which is evil, be afraid; for he bears not the sword in vain: for he is the minister of God, a revenger to execute wrath upon him that does evil. Wherefore ye must needs be subject, not only for wrath, but also for conscience sake. For for this cause pay ye tribute also: for they*

pp 209 / 226 /271

Cross-reference

Read *are God's ministers, attending continually upon this very thing. Render therefore to all their dues: tribute to whom tribute is due; custom to whom custom; fear to whom fear, honor to whom honor. Owe no man any thing, but to love one another: for he that loves another has fulfilled the law.*

Written in the bible chapters above lays out the bare rules for the governors and the governed in righteous leading and following according to the
GOVERNMENT OF GOD.
Each group following the commands, laws and ordinances of God displaying a hard stance of obedience and disobedience to the other.
This means all the different kinds of rulers, of governances will be accountable to the Lord this accountability will be measured by the right holy scriptures, the original King James Holy Bible, for within its pages bear witness of the many historical leaders, who despite how they ruled failed to bring about the perfect righteous rule, that put an end to all sufferings, pain, death, sickness, poverty etc.. **Matthew 24**..

pp 134 / 164 /71

Read *.. [**Matthew 24**]..in your original king James bible.* ***OKJB***

Any righteous rulers or government will strive for peace and prosperity for all its subjects, history tells us that this condition and position in this life is not going to become any where near a reality, though in itself is not a bad striving or goal, truth of the matter is however, rendering evil for evil to other men is not what God meant to bring about good..
1 Thessalonians 5:v15..

pg 5

Cross-reference

Wars and conflicts of all degrees and variants are the nature of mankind, brought about through its disobedience to God by the first man and woman and remains and evil to this day by propensity...**Genesis 3:v10-19**..

Read

***[1 Thessalonians 5:v15]**.. See that none render evil for evil unto any man; but ever follow that which is good, both among yourselves, and to all men. **[Genesis 3:v10-19]**.. Read all verses out from your* **OKJB.**

pg 130

Striving for this kind of career brings with it an antidote for right governance, a would be candidate for presidency or prime minister role usually kicks off with a series of campaigns promising a new better life for all, often bringing into the office of the new leader favoritisms, sorrow and suffering even war upon the very people voting for him or her these days, ignoring all the rules even the commands of the Almighty God, it's a tragedy that just will not go away in this life, Yet God said that He will make covenants with Governments, leaders even kings of nations that set their heart on Him through servants that he sends, Holy scripture bears testimony He will and has, however for those who don't, will lead and rule without His righteous rule and be held accountable for their own actions.. **1 Samuel 13:v14..**
2 Samuel 2v7.. And the Lord through His prophet Samuel tells king Saul that because he has done foolishly, he will be replaced by another king, that king was to be David, he had set his heart on God we can use the testimony of God and King David..

Cross-reference pg 60

Read *[**1 Samuel13:v14**].. But now thy kingdom shall not continue: the Lord hath sought Him a man after His own heart, and the Lord hath commanded him to be Captain over His people, because thou hast not kept that which the Lord commanded* **thee.**

Read *[**2 Samuel 2:v7**]. Therefore now let your hands be strengthened, and be valiant: For your master Saul is dead, and also the house of Judah have anointed me king over them.*

God is pleased and will support Governments, leaders, Kings even today when they strive to rule and reign in alignment with His commandments and laws, by abolishing all other forms of worship..**2 Kings 18:v4** He came to the earthly realm to fulfill the law or the prophets.. **Matthew 5:v17**

Read *[2 **Kings** 18:v4]. He removed the high places, and brake the images and cut down the groves, and brake down the brazen serpent that Moses had made: for unto those days the children of Israel did burn incense to it.. Read the full chapter in your original king James bible. [**Matthew 5:v17**]..Think not that I am come to destroy the law, or the prophets: I am not come to destroy, but to fulfill.*

pp 130 /100 /214 /29

However today its about spiritual wrestling and not war against flesh and blood, **Ephesians 6:v12** Its for this reason God came to the earthly realm to establish His kingdom of peace, a peace that is not because of the absence of war, but it is the absence of physical warfare, the war mentioned here is the war brought through the word, Jesus

Cross-reference

Christ gospel message which is sharper than any two edged sword which is to love God and neighbor as we love ourselves.. **Matthew10:v34...Matthew22:v37-39**..

Read *[**Ephesians 6:v12**]..For we wrestle not against flesh and blood, but against principalities, against powers against rulers of darkness of this world, against the spiritual wickedness in high places.*

pp 99/85

Read *..[**Matthew..10:v34**].. think not that I am come to send peace on earth: I came not to send peace but a sword..*

Read *..[**Matthew 22:v37-39**].. Jesus said unto him, Thou shalt love the Lord thy God with all thy heart, and with all thy soul, and with all thy mind. This is the first and great commandment. And the second is like unto it. Thou shalt love thy neighbor as thyself.*

pp 200 /269 /279

Jesus Christ had not come to remove governments, but to offer salvation to all mankind through them.. **Mark 16: v15**..
To those in the high places too, yet he will establish a rule of peace, a kingdom of peace established on earth.. **Daniel 2:v44**.. When this happens all other kingdoms will be no more, I tell a mystery; this kingdom is already here, no other Kingdom can overthrow it, there are already subjects or citizens, these have or are being prepared to dwell there having been called, excepted the invitation and made themselves ready.

Revelation 21:v2-4.. What world governments and leaders are failing to realize, failing to take notice of, is their forced rule of law, which is creating non sustainable societies, under the laws of man, its citizens are incarcerated and or imprisoned in trying to obey them, often instilling fear for law, which have become too

Cross-reference

numerous to keep without breaking those of the Lord, happening at the same time: these laws block even remove the feelings and emotions that people had been born with, even the conscience, how-ever by the abiding in the two fold command of love, Citizens to the Kingdom of God are made ready to inherit by the first choice to obey God and his laws and commands and not by force.

pp 117 /85 Read all *[**Mark16 :v15**]..and he said unto them, Go you into all the world, and preach the gospel to every creature..*

*[**Daniel 2:v44**].. and in the days of these Kings shall the God of heaven set up a kingdom.*

Which shall never be destroyed: and the kingdom shall not be left to other people, but it shall break in pieces and consume all these kingdoms, and it shall stand forever.

pp 74/181

*[**Revelation 21:v1-4**]..and I saw a new heaven and a new earth: for the first heaven and the first earth were passed away: and there was no more sea. And I John saw the holy city, new Jerusalem, coming down from God out of heaven, prepared as a bride adorned for her husband.*

NOTES

MOVEMENT NUMBER 21

Disfiguring the Body

Our body and life is not just ours.

Cross-reference

DISFIGURING THE BODY

The physical flesh and blood human body is more than just something a person is to use and do with as is pleased, a masterful complex of integrated components working together to achieve its purpose for being and that purpose is to know and honor its creator, for this to happen God the creator has put certain qualities and characteristics of Himself into the crown of his creation known as mankind or just man, which includes woman, in other words ***HIS IMAGE..*** **Genesis 1:v26/7**

Read ***[Genesis 1:v26-27]..*** *And God said, let us make man in our own image, after our likeness: and let them have dominion over the fish of the sea, and over the fowl of the air, and over the cattle, and over all the earth, and over every creeping thing that creeps upon the earth. So God created man in his own image, in the image of God created he him; male and female created he them.*

pp 176/ 189/ 201

This image and likeness is a chapter on its own, so I will concentrate on a few points, God the creator is pure and perfect, un defiled, the person of God is put into every human three parts:body soul and spirit, and at each conception, when the soul or life is formed, no physical body yet, just an invisible being, and that being is the image and likeness of God. However that image slowly starts to fade as a human physical body forms around it and human nature and character and influences become an attraction and lead to a

Cross-reference

defiling of all three. Before I get to some and how this happens I will share another biblical passage that tell mankind how we came into being formed out of the dust of the earth by someone else.. Man did not design and create or make himself.. **Genesis 2:v7**..

pg 276

Read *[**Genesis 2:v7**]..And the Lord God formed man of the dust of the ground, and breathed into his nostrils, the breath of life; and man became a living soul.*

And so; because of this truth and fact be warned that there will be serious eternal consequences should there be behaviors considered by God disregarding any kind of purposeful notion for having been given our own unique frames, spirit and soul, because what is done to one part effects the other two. This should be telling anyone reading this, I quote !! that my body, actually my life doesn't belong to me only, its partially owned by the creator of it, one can safely say.. borrowed or gifted me with it, and I should take good care of all of it preserving its form as it was at the beginning. No man has provided themselves with their body, the life and soul in it, not even one strand of hair. Lets find out what the biblical records say is not to be done too, in or on the flesh and skin covering the frame, recorded in.. **Leviticus 19:v26-28**..

Read *Ye shall not eat anything with the blood: neither shall ye use enchantment, nor observe times. Ye shall not round the corners of your heads, neither shalt thou mar the corners of thy beard. Ye shall not make any cuttings, in your flesh for*

Cross-reference

Read *the dead, nor print any marks on you: I am the Lord.. **[Leviticus 19:v26-28]**..*

The same voice that called this life into being is the same voice that commands what is NOT to be done to it and with it namely: No cuttings, No printing, No markings, there is no allowance given for cultures or rituals, not even for or to remember the dead, in this chapter, when God speaks He has spoken it is not for anyone to just go and do what they like and defile the purity of their body, no not for any reason or excuse, God will not be persuaded. Giving cause a title or a name does not change the no or the don't, not even conjuring up some fan dangled reason.. tattoos and earning a living providing for family will not change Gods will, His reproach will definitely follow, for these are his commands, to disobey God is foolish.. **Proverbs 18: v2-3**..

RR In ***Reality of Reality.*** . Our body and life is not just ours, for we did not create it.

Read ***[Proverbs 18:v2-3]**.. A fool hath no delight in understanding, but that his heart may discover itself. When the wicked cometh, then cometh also contempt, and with ignominy.*

Piercing the skin willfully for show, ritual, power and status etc has no part in a life with God, and no where is there recorded piercing the flesh to be a right act moreover an action that is associated with battle and the sword, to Jesus and His death by nailing, to the cross.. **Colossians 2:v14**..
and piercing His flesh.. **John 19:v34/37**..

Cross-reference

Read ***..[Colossians2:v14]**..Blotting out the handwriting of ordinances that was against us, which was contrary to us, and took it out of the way, nailing it to the cross.*

Read *..[**John 19:v34-37**].. But one of the soldiers with a spear pierced his side, and forthwith came there out blood and water. And he that saw it bare record and his record is true: and he knows that he saith true, that ye might believe. For these things were done, that the scripture should be fulfilled. A bone of him shall not be broken. And again another scripture saith, They shall look on him whom they have pierced.*

The Almighty creator God has given all mankind a body to temple His soul and spirit to house Him if you like..**1 Corinthians 6:v19-20**..It must be kept Holy, for the Holy Ghost to make its abode and where ever the body goes God goes too, He is witness to the ware abouts of every individual anywhere every time, witness to what has been done in that place and with whom, God's presence is omnipresent meaning He is everywhere at the same time all of the time.. **Proverbs 15:v3** He is watching, His eyes are watching the evil and the good.

[**1 Corinthians 6:v19-20**]..What? Know ye not that your body is the temple of the Holy Ghost which is in you, which ye have of God (those whom have received the Holy Ghost only) and ye are not your own? For ye are bought with a price :therefore glorify God in your body, and in your spirit, which are God's. [**Proverbs 15:v3**]..The eyes of the Lord are in every place, beholding the evil and the good.

Cross-reference

This body is to be nurtured in every sense, it is to be kept in good health, in a fit state both physically and spiritually the mind should be vigilant, learning as time goes, growing and developing taking out of and from the many events and lessons of life, more over learning about the Almighty God, this should be the common practices of everyone, come rain or shine for all people of all races, cultures and statures, the same written above is the same for all.. **Romans 2:v11**

Read *For there is no respect of persons with God. **[Romans 2:v11]**..*

pp 32/235

And so defiling can take place on the seen out side and on the unseen inside, yet God knows because He looks at the heart as everything is manifest through the spiritual heart of man.. **Proverbs 23:v7**.. Defiling also comes about by what goes in through spiritual means such as.. Evil Music, false teachings, movies or pictures having a violent or pornographic content that cause participation in the mind and or physical.. **Matthew 15:v18-20**.. and should be avoided, as too should be the excessive taking of drugs.

Read *For as he thinks in his heart, so is he......*

Read ***[Proverbs23:v7]**..Portion.*
But those things which proceed out the mouth come forth from the heart; and they defile the man. For out of the heart proceed evil thoughts, murders, adulteries, fornications, thefts, false witness, blasphemies. These are the things which defile a man:but to eat with unwashed hands defiles not a man.
..[Matthew 15:v18-20]..

REALITY *of* ***REALITY***

MOVEMENT NUMBER 22

One More Thing

There will always be one more thing to be done, choose, and do.

Cross-reference

ONE MORE THING

There is always one more thing to be done, to sit back and think! I have done it all, I have everything I need, everything I want, as high as I can go, I'm at the top I have built my fortress, castle be it status, wealth, power, or that real heavy duty fortress and expect to always be safe and secure, behind them there high stone walls and battlements, is pure folly, because effectively that is not the real end there will come another time, when its time to leave that fortress, that castle, that status, power all that has been accumulated in this world of flesh and blood, I am giving reference to death of the body that one more thing, and depart from this world, leaving behind all those earthly treasures, yet this is not the end, there is still one more thing to be done. I use two stories from the Holy bible, one story tells of a people shut up in the fortress of Jericho, no one is going out or coming in and the other tells of a farmer who had a bumper harvest and thought to himself that he was positioned so well that he would knock down his existing barns just to build bigger ones, sit down and relax as if nothing more to do. These two stories do not find favor with the Lord, and thus God shows in these two scenes that God should be sought as the one more thing. The story of Jericho.. **Joshua 6..** tells that the inhabitants wanted to rule themselves live as they wanted, and so built this impregnable fortress, none went out and none came in. God instructed Joshua his servant to invade this defiant people and overthrow the fortress, kill all therein.. **v21**.. everyone accept the household of Rehab **v22/3**..The story is extraordinary, God

Cross-reference

commands the whole matter. His word was to be final for this matter, yet there will still be one more thing and that one thing is to except and follow Jesus Christ or reject Him.

Read *All of [**Joshua chapter 6**] in your original king James bible.* ***OKJB***

Read *The other story is a parable, an earthly story with a heavenly meaning, Jesus taught this way so that it would separate the believers from the non believers.* ***Luke 12:v16-21****..*

pp 244 /280 /294

Read *And he spake a parable unto them saying, The ground of a certain rich man brought fourth plentifully: And he thought within himself, saying, What shall I do because I have no room where to bestow my fruits and my goods. And I shall say to my soul, Soul, thou hast much goods laid up for many years; take thine ease, eat, drink, and be merry. But God said unto him. Thou fool, this night thy soul shall be required of thee: then whose shall those things be, which thou hast provided? So is he that lays up treasure for himself, and is not rich toward God.* ***[Luke 12 :v16-21]****..*

RR The ***Reality of Reality*** is until the absolute end, humans still have that freedom of choice, One more thing then in these illustrations would be carried over into the spiritual life, yet one can put it this way.. one life line has been lost to the earthly life, and now the other life, the life in the spirit becomes real choice is real, the second life line. At this first death all of the above now becomes the opposite, actually the same

Cross-reference

meaning all the worldly gaining, the looking after the natural life leaves the once earthly rich, now spiritually poor, bound in spiritual poverty, with no treasures having been stored up in heaven through choice.. **Mark 10:v21** .One more thing, now becomes one more big thing, this is a serious situation to be found in, having chosen to be locked up inside this great big fortified fortress hidden behind the huge walls, assuming that no one could see and interfere with the happenings going on there, were mistaken, foolish, God knew all along, He knew that it was the right thing to do to expose this evil existence not just for the inhabitants sake only, but for all mankind that would come after. This seemingly secure and carefree lifestyle under the auspices of a life devoid of any consequences let alone spiritual, was not to be, this image for prosperity has revealed itself to the reality of spiritual poverty, quite the opposite.

Read

[Mark 10:v21]..*Then Jesus beholding him loved him, and said unto him, One thing thou lack: go thy way, sell what thou hast, and give to the poor, and thou shalt have treasure in heaven: and come, take up thy cross and follow me.*

And so the two earthly life accounts lived and one life line used, now reveal an Unprepared, without help; having skipped past some very invaluable spiritually one more things offered whilst in the body, things that still have to be undone, still to be settled, like paying a debt one cannot just skip a payment just to expect it be forgotten, NO! those missed one last things still

Cross-reference

can be settled, now a type of spiritual account that should be reduced to a nil balance by that one more thing called choice, choose the Lord and wipe everything away, or the evil one and the debt will remain. For those who choose to obey the Lord Jesus Christ as their one more thing done in the body, will of course be the willingness to follow him, and in so doing will choose that the last supper meal they will eat will be his body and blood through the sacrament of holy communion. **Matthew 26:v26-28** having presumably had as the last meal on earth for the body, the last one for the soul now becomes a one more thing to be done.

pg 54 Read *[**Matthew 26:v26-28**].. And as they were eating, Jesus took bread, and blessed it and brake it, and gave it to the disciples, and said. Take eat: this is my body. And he took the cup, and gave thanks, and gave it to them, saying, Drink ye all of it. For this is my blood of the new testament, which is shed for many for the remission of sins.*

One more thing, to hear the message of the cross, this will happen, or would have happened yet was or was not taken serious, if it had, the immediate action to take would be to cry out to hear it some more, to hear more about it, this will be acknowledgment of the state or condition the soul and spirit is in and desire be helped, a bowing down is required in recognition to Jesus Christ sacrificial death and resurrection made through the sign of the cross, this one thing has to be completed willingly.. **Isaiah 45:v23**. The Gospel of Jesus Christ has to be preached to every soul that has been created by God, to

Cross-reference

all the corners of the world, everywhere for all times.. **Matthew 28:v19-20**..

Read

*[**Isaiah 45:v23**]..I have sworn by myself, the word is gone out of my mouth in righteousness, and shall bow, every tongue shall swear.. [**Matthew 28:v19-20**]. Go ye therefore, and teach all nations, baptizing them in the name of the Father and of the son, and of the holy Ghost: Teaching them to observe all things whatsoever I have commanded you: and, lo, I am with you always, even unto the end of the world. Amen.*

pp 36 /184

ONE MORE THING : Boils down to a single choice, followed by the appropriate action, there are only two choices or two ways, one leading to eternal rest and peace, whereas the other way will lead to eternal wrestling and no peace, Jesus is the first way and the devil is the other. Both ways have been revealed here, as with any journey passing through a door is the beginning, Jesus is the door to freedom and green pastures, through this door there is light, which is life, and this door no one can shut. The other door leads to darkness and death which no one can re-open, after passing through it. The door is an image of choices made during ones two life lines, as described above, everyone has been shown by their choice which way they are going, all the directions and requirements would have made available during the earth life line and the spiritual life line, and so the choice would have been made and done as the final one last thing ending at the final judgment.. **Revelation 20:v12**..Jesus is the door.. **John 10:v9**..

pg 271

Read

*[**Revelation 20:v12**]..And I saw the dead, small and great, stand before God; and the books were*

Cross-reference

Read *opened: and another book was opened, which is the book of life another: and the dead were judged out of those things which were written in the books, according to their works.*

Read ***[John 10:v9]****.. I am the door: by me if any man enter in, he shall be saved, and shall go in and out, and find pasture.*

NOTES

REALITY *of* ***REALITY***

MOVEMENT NUMBER 23

Automation

Automation will bring automated sickness and diseases to man's heart and mind.

Cross-reference

AUTOMATION

RR

The ***reality of Reality*** is this : Automation does not exist in this life, nothing happens on its own, or automatically, when God created the heavens and the earth, on the seventh day He had finished His work and rested.. **Genesis 2: v2**..

Read

And on the seventh day, God ended his work which he had made; and he rested on the seventh day from all his work which he had made.. ***[Genesis 2:v2]***..

pg 260

Literally! we can't take the word or term DAY, it could be many years, centuries even many centuries a span man is not able to fathom..**1 Corinthians 1: 19-21**..

Read

[1 Corinthians 1:v19-21].. *For it is written, I will destroy the wisdom of the wise and bring to nothing the understanding of the prudent.. Where is the wise? where is the scribe? Where is the disputer of this world? Hath God not made the foolish the wisdom of this world?..For after that in the wisdom of God the world by wisdom knew not God, it pleased God by the foolishness of preaching to save them that believe.*

And so automation plants are by man for man, there are numerous reasons for this, as a starting point, the root of all evil is money, with the world population expounding exponentially, obviously there is at least according to the wisdom of man, money to be made out of producing more products with less cost by using robotics, governments allow this because out of the process lots of tax is also generated,

Cross-reference

providing more power through the money, to become stronger in other areas such as in military robotics can be set to operate 24 hours per day, 7 days per week, every day of the year. The focus is "MONEY".. **1 Timothy 6:v10** Despite the consequences can be fatal, because the laws and commandments of God will be transgressed by all participating.. **James 2:v10**..

Read

pp 120/238

pg 29

*[**1 Timothy 6:v10**].. For the love of money is the root of all evil: Which while some coveted after, they have erred from the faith, and pierced themselves through with many sorrows..[**James 2:v10**]..For whosoever shall keep the whole law, and yet offend in one point, he is guilty of all.*

Nature in itself is a prime example that nothing is automatic, new life a baby coming into the world, from the time of conception taking a further 9 months to grow and develop within the womb of the mother, before being born as a fully formed human, some creatures or insects go through a metamorphism a complete transformation from one condition to another, for example a caterpillar into a butterfly, animals that Hibernate for months at a time, sleeping as if still !.. to emerge from an almost non existent state, just to carry on with its life, to carry on where it left off. The promised one that would bruise the head of the serpent [the devil].. Goes back thousands of years.. **Genesis 3:v15**.. Yet that promise has been fulfilled in Jesus Christ.. **Matthew 2:v11**.. time is proof enough that nothing is auto. Christ Himself as man, was subject to time, "yet one person of the triune God" a perfect example of this is found in one of His miracles.. **Mark 8:v22-25**.

Cross-reference

The promise of this Messiah Jesus Christ to return or make another appearance has been made 2020 plus years ago, yet still to be fulfilled, this will happen after the many signs have come to the fore.. **Matthew 24**..

Read *__[Genesis 15:v15]__.. And I will put enmity between thee and the woman, and between thy seed and her seed; it shall bruise thy head, and thou shalt bruise his heel... __[Matthew 2:v11]__.. And when they were come into the house, they saw the young child with Mary his mother, and fell down, and worshiped him: and when they presented him gifts; gold, frankincense and myrrh. __[Mark8:v22-25]__..And he cometh to Beth-sa'i-da: and they bring a blind man unto him, and besought him to touch him. And he took the blind man by the hand and led him out of the town; and when he had spit on his eyes, and put his hands upon him, he ask him if he saw ought. And he looked up and said, I see men as trees, walking. After that he put his hands again upon his eyes, and made him look up: and he was restored, and saw every man clearly. Read..__[Matthew 24]__ in your original king James bible as you like. __OKJB__*

pg 5

pp 134 /141 /71

These testimonies reveal that God is not in automation. Another example refuting that automation does not come from the creator God is in the truth that each human, that every person is an individual, having personalized characteristics such as finger prints and DNA blood types and skin markings hair follicles that separates one person from an other, or race through genealogy technologies making identification to certain events in life traceable down to a single person, paving away for an all

Cross-reference

conclusive judgment of no doubt possible, this is the will of God. Automation is an invention out of the folly of man, in a human effort by man to cover up errors derived or coming out of his disobedience to the commands of and nature of God, a general trend that is growing across most, if not all sectors of the world, high profiled people, governments and leaders, royalty, church leaders, teachers, parents and individuals, seemingly with none or little opposition, yet any person realizing this as evil practice, is to avoid becoming directly involved in such practice.

Stripping God's beloved creation of person to person contact will not go unseen by the all present all knowing God.. **Psalm 139**.. Nowhere will be a hiding place; for God is in all of heaven and even in all of hell, already there are signs of a disappointed loving creator emerging within the human race known simply as Autism, accepted by people as just another weakness or disease that has come upon them and their children.. **Numbers 14:v18**..

pg 204

Read *[**Psalm 139**].. Read all of this Psalm out of your original king James bible. **OKJB***

Read *The Lord is long suffering, and of great mercy, forgiving iniquity and transgression and by no means clearing the guilty, visiting the iniquity, of the fathers upon the children unto the third and fourth generation..[**Numbers 14:v18**]..*

This above in the colored box is evidence that so called automation practices are evil and over time will be bring great tribulations and sorrows, which already is

Cross-reference

revealing itself through this disease aptly named Autism, a medical term for a relatively new disorder rearing its ugly head amidst children Governments and world authorities even churches are failing to seek the Glory (help) of the Almighty God amidst this constant increase in the worlds human population draws them

RR

closer and closer to the scientists and advisers, that in the ***Reality of Reality*** pushes humankind further away fro m God and His absolute will, and the nations will rush into things, like the rushing of mighty waters without consulting to even considering God's will first or at all, most certainly.

He will rebuke them.

Isaiah 17:v10-14..

Read

Because you have forgotten the God of your salvation, and have not been mindful of the rock of thy strength, therefore shalt thou plant pleasant plants, and shalt set it with strange ships: In the day shalt thou make thy seed to flourish: but the harvest shall be a heap in the day of grief and of desperate sorrow. Woe to the multitude of many people, which make a noise of the seas: and to the rushing of nations, that make a rushing like the rushing of mighty waters! The nations shall rush like the rushing of many waters : but God shall rebuke them, and they shall flee far off, and shall be chased as the chaff of the mountains before the wind, and like a rolling thing before the whirlwind.. ***[Isaiah 17:v10-14]***..

REALITY *of* ***REALITY***

MOVEMENT NUMBER 24

The Life in the Next Life

A life with Jesus Christ is total freedom. Without him, total bondage.

Cross-reference

THE LIFE IN THE NEXT LIFE

The next life is real, as real as this first one this is the life we as humans live out on the earth, a life with body and blood; the next life with no body and blood is the life we as humans will live after leaving the earth, a life in the spirit with no flesh and blood. Our total or complete life incorporates the human part and the spiritual part its impossible to separate these two parts in this life, that happens at the first death yet the part that dominates will be the dominant one in that next life, a kind of tussle takes place, between the desires of the human body and those of the soul and spirit, after the physical body goes back to the earth and out of the way, the soul and spirit remains. How this first life is lived by choice will be the same lived in the next life, every person should come to this knowledge of truth, that what is done now or today has good or bad consequences for tomorrow, the future. The worst choice anyone can make is to deny Jesus Christ to be whom the biblical records of the many the witnesses claim him to be.. God incarnate or the son of God, however best it is for our understanding..1 **John 4:v15**..To enter the next life with this disposition is as good as having no light at all, no warmth, no comfort or direction total chaos and confusion, it's a prison type state of being, all possibilities of goodness will not be found within for that gift of choice is removed, all goodness and light can only come from the outside, a friend, neighbor or relative, servant of the Lord those whom follow Christ to Jesus himself..

Acts 12: 5-7..

Cross-reference

pg 58

pg 246

Read *[1 John 4:v15]..Whosoever shall confess that Jesus is the Son of God. God dwell in him, and he in God.* ***[Acts 12: v5-7]****..Peter therefore was kept in prison: but prayer was made without ceasing of the church unto God for him. And when Herod would have brought him forth, the same night Peter was sleeping between two soldiers, bound with two chains:and the keepers before the door kept the prison. And behold the angel of the Lord came upon him, and a light shined in the prison: and he smote Peter on the side, and raised him up, saying Arise up quickly. And his chains fell off from off from his hands. Read the full chapter in your original king James bible.* ***OKJB***

Life beyond the grave is spiritual the soul and spirit of the deceased person will continue life in the spirit world, the beyond or heavenly realm, they all refer to life in the next life, the grave will now become the resting place meaning where it stops, yet not just as simple nor just as welcoming as it sounds, nope, in that grave is the world of the dead, everything that drove the life of that person, the spirits he/she served the worldly lusty spirits that now become its master and can be quite terrifying on that side, perhaps even bondage, this will of course depend on the lifestyle lived out in the body, determined by choices/rejections made.. **Luke 16:v19-31**..

pp 76/25 /28/278/245

Read ***[Luke 16:v19-31]****.. Read all these verses from your original king James bible.* ***OKJB***

Rejecting Jesus Christ after having been introduced to Him, will mean bondage trapped in the spirits served whilst on the earth, a life of greed, of selfish living a controlling nature, lies

Cross-reference

and deceit, wickedness, a know all nobody can tell me anything kind of character, I reckon you get the Jist? be sure that on the other side those spirits will be at you, non stop they will keep you fighting, those in this state will have no rest and no peace.. **John 8:v24**.. For rejecting Christ means to die in ones own sins, those sins will be reflected and felt in the constant torment of those spirits, no one gets away with anything, there is accountability.

Read

***[John 8:v24]**..I said therefore unto you, that ye die in your sins: for if ye believe not that I am he, ye shall die in your sins.*

The next life, I am calling heaven, the yonder or spirit world heaven refers to above or below but out of the earth realm, it is a heavenly spirit kingdom where nothing can be touched as can be done in the earth realm, yet an exact replica there are buildings, roads, cars, trains, hills, rivers, churches, prisons of course people bars clubs etc, however having said this, those whom have rejected Jesus will be bound to their graves, which has become their spiritual prison a result of their serving of evil spirits, they cannot leave or come and go, unlike the saints those who accepted and followed Jesus can come out of theirs, in the same way that one can come in and go out of their earthly home as it pleased them **Matthew 27:v52/53**..

Read

***[Matthew 27:v52/53]**..And the graves were opened: and many bodies of the saints which slept arose. And came out of the graves after his resurrection and went into the holy city, and appeared unto many.*

Cross-reference

RR

Because the ***Reality of Reality*** what happens in either realm works the same, the name of Jesus is also spread freely in heaven, those that followed Christ and spread his good news gospel message on earth, which is to those that accept and follow him on earth, though they shall die they will also live and be free of the power of sin which is death, will not be bound to their graves and so can continue to spread the good news message of the cross just as they believed and did in all the freedom that comes by accepting the life, death and resurrection of Jesus Christ.. **Revelation 1:v18** Through choice by choice, NO forcing, Jesus was not forced to go to the cross no human is forced to accept or follow

Read

*[**Revelation 1:v18**]..I am he that liveth, and was dead; and behold, I am alive forevermore, Amen; and have the keys of hell and of death.*

pg 85

This life is mirrored in the next life in terms of the spiritual, for example: when one acts out according to their thought, the action that follows becomes the end result of a spiritual motivation, this can be for the right or wrong reason and will be recorded as so in the soul of that person, to be transferred into the next life be it good or evil, thus will free or bind.

NOTES

REALITY *of* ***REALITY***

MOVEMENT NUMBER 25

There is Always an Original

One original. Many fakes.

Cross-reference

THERE IS ALWAYS AN ORIGINAL

Yes though there are many fakes, copies, untruths, out there in this big vast world, there is also the original to everything the real McCoy, the right one and the truth. When something first comes out, it is the original, be it a painting, car, an animal every human, male or female, the word of the Lord which is the bible, the church that Jesus built: on this rock I will build my church.. **Matthew 16:v18**.. The first the original ...Yet because the world is big and the population is many there has to be reproductions of the original, to supply all wanting.. Like the car, the bible. NOW !! There are Churches by the thousands with hundreds opening up around the globe each year offering a solution for every want or need for that person or family, should things not work out in one, simply go to another and another, one door closes another opens as the saying goes, what really could stand in the way of looking for a church that gives what is wanted, even though it may be fake or speak any heresies for some that's what is wanted and just good enough. There is an original church, it still exists, it will not go away, it's complete having everything the church is to have by the standards of its designer in fulfilling the purpose it is intended, That purpose is to join all the members [people] of the church into one body of believers, after having come under the same teaching, counsel, one truth all working together for the edifying of each other. The church lends its origin in the kingdom of God, manifesting in fulfilled promises, miracles and wonders formulating the information necessary

Cross-reference

to establish the solid foundation upon which the church would be built upon...**Colossians 1:v24**..

Read

pp 182 /220 /132 /36

[Matthew 16:v18]..*And I say also unto thee, That thou art Peter, and upon this rock, I will build my church; and the gates of hell shall not prevail against it.* ***[Colossians 1:v24]*** *Who now rejoice in my sufferings for you, and fill up that which is behind of the afflictions of Christ in my flesh for his body's sake, which is the church.*

Of course when we refer to church we mean the members, joined into one body not the name or the building, these will be left behind or lost to the earthly.

Thus we come to the **Original King James Holy Bible**, compiled out of and from the original scrolls written in either Hebrew or Greek and so have been translated from these original tongues into different languages as close as possible if not perfectly interpreted to bring the actual moments to life in all languages and tongues. Preserved for the purpose of providing the information that would be used in authenticating it's originality, I'm convinced the **original King James version bible** printed in **1611**, translated by **47 scholars** and theologians over **7 years** is the bible God had known would be that part of His church even before the creation of heaven and earth. The Almighty God is not confused and cannot confuse anyone, it would not be righteous for Him to have different variations of bibles, certainly there are differences, some very noticeable and should be avoided, my counsel here is to rather put more effort into learning

Cross-reference

from the original right bible in your desired language and not deviate, with prayer and hard work it has all that the Almighty God has preserved for a life pleasing to Him. Something that I have considered adds to its authenticity the original king James holy bible from any other is the stern warning incorporated at the end **Revelations.. 22:v18 and v19**..

Read

*For I testify unto every man that hears the words of the prophecy of this book, if any man shall add unto these things, God shall add unto him the plagues that are written in this book. And if any man shall take away from the words of this prophecy, God shall take away his part out of the book of life, and out of the holy city, and from the things that are written in this book..**[Revelation 22:v18+19]**..*

pg 1

You the reader and I the writer and every human being is an original, none of us are copies of another, we can add more, the sun, moon are originals, the earth is one of a kind, its animals, creatures every one after its own kind, created by this same Almighty God in His word, Himself an original, there is and can only be one Jesus Christ the son of God and man, these are living proof that originals do exists.. **Genesis 1:v25**..

pp 189/201

Read

[Genesis 1:v21-25]v22** and God created great whales, and every living creature that moves, which the waters brought forth abundantly, after their kind, and every winged fowl after its kind: and God saw that it was good, read to **v25** from original king James bible. **OKJB

Cross-reference

The original we are focusing on here is not the original source of all wrongs, the opposite; the original source of all that is right, all that is true born out of love that source is in and from the Almighty triune God, creator of heaven and earth. Passed on through the word in His only begotten son Jesus Christ.. **John 1:v1-5** then on through the outpouring of the Holy spirit, yet by so much more, His Bible the original testaments old and new, the creation, the Lord of Host's, his servants at this culmination of information let it be known that this original truth can not disappear nor lose any of its power, as the source He will preserve all of it for all time, because the source the Almighty God is the information found in the words it is all Him and he is all of

RR it.. and its all in this ***Reality of Reality*** book.

Read *In the beginning was the Word, and the Word was with God, and the Word was God. The same was in the beginning with God. All things were made by him; and without him was not anything made that was made. In him was life; and the life was the light of men. And the light shines in darkness; and the darkness comprehended it not..**[John 1:v1-5]**..*

pp 40 /284

NOTES

REALITY *of* ***REALITY***

MOVEMENT NUMBER 26

A Named Church

The church of Christ has no name IT is hidden in the word of God.

Cross-reference

A NAMED CHURCH

Has Jesus Christ put a name and emblem to identify his church on the earth? or is it just Identified through his Gospel message with the Old and New Testaments to authenticate IT. Certainly in my **OKJB** there is no indication of such an identity.. with so many named organization churches, religious denominations in the world today with each one professing to be the right one, to the point of claiming to heal sicknesses, cast out demons, give life to the

RR

deceased, the ***Reality of Reality*** these are deceptions, so where does a sinner seeking a changed life go? My experience has shown me that it is with God and Christ whom is called to the salvation plan, He will answer prayers and reveal His real church through grace but it will be up to the individual to accept the call, and follow.

Matthew 7:v22-23..will reveal itself when Jesus words come true: I never knew you depart from me for his real church is none of them, for IT is within.. IT, Jesus church is made alive by the Holy Spirit **1 Corinthians 3:v16-18**..

Read

*[**Matthew 7:v22-23**]..Many will say to me in that day, Lord, Lord have we not prophesied in thy name? and in thy name cast out devils? and in thy name done many works?.. And then will I profess unto them, I never knew you: depart from me, ye that work iniquity.*

Read

*..[**1 Corinthians 3:v16-18**].. Know you not that you are the temple of God, and that the spirit of God dwells in you? If any man defile the temple of God, him shall God destroy; for the temple of God is holy, which temple ye are. Let no man deceive himself, If any man among you seems to be wise in this world, let him become a fool, that he may be wise.*

Cross-reference

This is worth mentioning: that at the end of the time of grace the church of Christ will be the spiritual body of believers called the tabernacle is with men. **Revelation 21:v3**..No other name, physical building but the word of life which is Jesus Christ dwelling in this spiritual body of many members (believers) these are overcomer's or known as saints.

Read

pg 74

[Revelation 21:v3] *And I heard a great voice out of heaven saying, Behold, the tabernacle of God is with men, and he will dwell with them, and they shall be his people, and God himself will be with them, and be their God.*

Emblems even if bearing the sign of the cross are not bad or wrong at a first glance, certainly for some accepted in faith, yet behind the seemingly innocence lurks a potential evil that if not recognized could lead to idol worship simply by promoting the emblem for other types of gain by leaders or higher powers within the authority position. Many churches use the motive; fundraising to enrich themselves becoming servers of God and mammon.. **Matthew 6:v24** often drawing their faithful members into performing this very first punishable evil that God hates.. **Hosea 13:v4**..

pp 293 /241 /228

Read

*..**[Matthew 6:v 24]**.. No man can serve two masters: for either he will hate the one and love the other; or else he will hold to the one, and despise the other, ye cannot serve God and mammon..**[Hosea 13:v4]**..Yet I am the Lord thy God from the Land of Egypt, and thou shalt know no god but me: for there is no savior beside me.*

Cross-reference

Church is the people symbolizing members of a body working together by the command of the head which is Jesus Christ, these commands are the words of His Gospel coming through to the members similar to messages reaching body parts in a person through the human nerve system.. **1 Corinthians 12:v12-27** Church "the people" will come out from different bodies or denominations as chosen and led to Jesus by His Father God.. **John 6:v44**.. Just as no person has picked who they are: male or female, white or colored, when they entered the earthly realm through birth, so no one has picked themselves to be joined to this body of members.. the church of Jesus Christ.. **Matthew 16:v18**.. But the Almighty God for no one comes to me unless my Father draws him, words of Jesus.

Read

[**1 Corinthians 12 :v12-27**]..Read all verses from your original king James bible they describe the church as a body with many members, just as a human has a head, body and members or body parts joined and working together.

pg 132

Read

*[**Matthew 16:v18**]..And I say also unto thee, That thou art Peter, and upon this rock I will build my church; [**John 6:v44**]..No man can come to me except the Father which hath sent me draw him: and I will raise him up at the last day,*

pp 220 /175 /132 /36

Jesus true church is set apart from all others by the Holy altar.. **Revelation 6:v9**.. and what takes place there, these are Holy Acts, acts of grace performed by living apostles, ordinary men called by Jesus, it is at this holy altar that both the living and the dead must come to by kneeling to receive grace.. **Philippians 2:v10-11**..

Read about these Holy Acts [sacraments] in the book of the Acts of the Apostles, for there are three that bear record on earth: water, spirit, blood, they are Holy: Baptism, Sealing, Communion. **Acts 8:v17**..

Cross-reference

To call his church [members] together, Jesus first called out some fishermen to take up their cross [suffering] and follow him, saying; I will make you fishers of men these men were to become his disciples, staying close to and learning from him going on to become his ambassadors /apostles and given the famous great commission: saying: Go you therefore and teach, make disciples of all nations.. **Matthew 28:v19-20**.. this commission was given to the **12** and still alive and active in the same discipleship and apostle ministry today, and some other ministries to assist them.. **Ephesians 4:v11**.. continuing until the Lord comes, this will signify the end of this grace period once the Gospel has been preached to all nations.. **Matthew24:v14**..

And so the markers as to the exact location on earth of the one true holy altar bearing the sign of the cross [suffering] has to have all **7** components mentioned.. these are: Jesus [word] apostolate [ministry[three sacraments, holy altar and the member body [church].

pg 79

Read *..**[Revelation 6:v9]**.. And when he had opened the fifth seal, I saw under the altar the souls of them that had been slain for the word of God, and for the testimony which they held..*

*..**[Matthew 10:v2]**..Now the names of the twelve apostles are these:* ***READ ALL CHAPTER 10 .. ..***

pg 242

pp 30/93

Read *[**Ephesians 4:v11**].. And he gave some apostles; and some evangelists, and some pastors and teachers.. **[Acts 8:v17]**.. Then laid they their hands on them and they received the Holy Ghost.*

*..**[Philippians 2v10-11]**..That at the name of Jesus every knee should bow, of things in heaven, and things in earth, and things under the earth. And that every tongue should confess that Jesus Christ is Lord, to the Glory of God the Father.*

When you are called, that call you will know it choose to bow down and accept.

Cross-reference

Read

..*[**Matthew 24:v14**]..And this gospel of the kingdom shall be preached in all the world for a witness unto all nations; and then shall the end come.*

Coming back to a named church meaning; having a registered title by compliance and bound by or under governments rules, laws and legislation as amended from time to time, and why I no more hold to that title or name to be one in the physical and spiritual workings as it was with the gospel teachings of Jesus Christ in his day, the workings of the original church of Christ and holy acts of the first apostles, in all aspects and matters such as financial through offerings / donations, to taking care of the orphans and widows, to managing and the appointing of and the canceling of ministry, and hierarchy status, again I have learned that the temptation to miss manage by the wrong use of authority to favoritism and showing partiality through compliance or non compliance will always be there.. **Matthew 13:v30** ..yet Jesus true church he will preserve..

pp 36 /158

Matthew 16:v18.. IT will come from many named churches, from different ways of life, his sheep are in different folds, is the picture, after all.. what counts is faith, when Jesus returns, will he find faith

Read

Matthew 13:v30].. *Let both grow together until harvest: and in the time of harvest I will say to the reapers, first the tares and bind them into bundles, to burn them: but gather the wheat into my barn.*

Read

*And the gates of hell shall not prevail against it. [**Matthew 16:v18***

Though Jesus church activities did cease around 80 AD after the first apostles were killed or died of old age and the full

Cross-reference

activity of the holy spirit linked with the apostle ministry lapsed, all would be revived and start up again in the late 1800s, [always two] after some clergymen of catholic background got together in Scotland and prayed for the second out pouring of the holy spirit together with the re awakening of the apostle ministry that Jesus real church [body of believers] could begin to reassemble as one body from around the world as would happen told by Jesus Christ and the prophets.. **Matthew 28:v19-20**.. **Joel 2:v23..** it would be identified by the name New Apostolic Church. ***More on this NAC in RR book two.***

RR book two

Read ***..[Matthew 28:v19-20]..*** *Go you therefore, and teach all nations, baptizing them in the name of the Father, and of the son, and of the holy ghost: Teaching the to observe all things whatsoever I have commanded you: and lo I am with you alway, even unto the end of the world.*

Jesus actual church should not be confused with a physical building, which cannot endure, name or emblem, it is people laboring together in spirit..**1 Corinthians 3:v9 -11** called and joined together by the holy spirit, in the light of the Gospel of Jesus Christ, to build one faith on one baptism, the apostle ministry is an instrument God uses to bring these gifts together, these apostle men are to act in complete unity with the ministry as is written in **OKJB,** receiving the same instructions and works as the first apostles did that were called by Christ.

The danger comes in when the church leaders put too much emphasis on the physical by using a name /emblem to attract monetary wealth.. **Mark 11:v17..**to the extent of building impressive structures.. A WARNING TO LEADERS.

Jesus church is within, built on the belief of the resurrection of Jesus..

Read **[Joel 2:v23]..[1 Corinthians 3:v9-11]..[Mark 11:v17]** from your **OKJB.**

NOTES

REALITY *of* ***REALITY***

MOVEMENT NUMBER 27

Same-Sex Relationships

God changes not, mankind has to choose too

Cross-reference

SAME-SEX RELATIONSHIPS

I will say from this point on, I am writing this from the standpoint that there is no good or right for me in this type of behavior, I have to put this wrong in the same category as any other wrong or the breaking of any one of the Lord's ten commandments..

Deuteronomy chapter 5..and has to be overcome no matter what it takes, it is a temptation to sin by the evil one, I believe that God will help to over come, for with God there will be a way of escape, because as with any sin, it leads to death and eternal separation from Him, He does not wish that.**1 Corinthians 10:v13.. Romans 6:v23..**

Read *[**Deuteronomy chapter 5**].. Read the entire chapter from your original king James bible.* ***OKJB***

Read *There hath no temptation taken you but such as is common to man: but God is faithful, who will not suffer you to be tempted above that ye are able; but will make a way to escape, that ye may be able to bear it..**[1Corinthians10:v13]** **[Romans 6:v23]**..For the wages of sin is death; but the gift of God is eternal life through Jesus Christ our Lord.*

pg 281

I will add to the above, that God will have the final say and so this is not the end of the story: for every case is different. God made male and female to compliment each other in serving their creator through a right relationship, therefore the merging of their bodies into one flesh made possible through the way they have been created.. **Genesis 2:v24/5**.Be fruitful and multiply says the Lord as He instills the gift of reproduction in

Cross-reference

them, replenish the earth He says, have children give life out of thy life, gather a loving family together, be true and faithful to each other, remember where you have come from.. **Genesis 1:v27/8**.. at this point all was right and good, the couple only knew goodness to be naked felt right and good, having children was a pleasure it was right, no reason to have any other thought or notions.

Read *[**Genesis 2:v24-25**]..Therefore shall a man leave his father and his mother, and shall cleave to his wife: and they shall be one flesh..*

pg 212

pp 148/201

*[**Genesis 1:v27-28**]..So God created man in his own image, in the image of God created he him; male and female created he them. And God blessed them, and God said unto them, Be fruitful and multiply, and replenish the earth, and subdue it: and have dominion over the fish of the sea, and over the fowl of the air, and over every living thing that moves upon the earth..*

There is no mention of man and man or woman and woman, its impossible to be one flesh like this, there is no way children can come out of such relationships a family, God has destroyed cities for committing such acts: homosexual / lesbian defying HIM, His very nature his image and commandments, no such behavior will He accept nor forgive, it has to be overcome, that's all there is to it. [**Genesis 19:v24-29**]..

Read *[**Genesis 19:v24-29**]..Then the Lord rained upon Sodom and upon Go-mor-rah brimstone and fire from the Lord out of heaven; And he overthrew those cities, and all the plain, and all the inhabitants of the cities, and that which*

Cross-reference

Read

grew upon the ground. But his wife looked back from behind him, and she became a pillar of salt. And Abraham got up early in the morning to the place where he stood before the Lord: And he looked toward Sodom and Go-mor'rah, and toward all the land of the plain, and beheld, and, lo, the smoke of the the country went up as the smoke of a furnace. And it came to pass, when God destroyed the cities of the plain, that God remembered Abraham, and sent Lot out of the midst of the overthrow, when he overthrew the cities in the which Lot dwelt. Read all of ***chapter 19*** *in your original king James bible.* ***OKJB***

Up unto the first married man and woman Adam and Eve, the creation and life in the garden of Eden was good until they succumbed to the very first temptation committing the first sin as recorded in.. **Genesis chapter 3**.. Life was right just the way God the creator had created it, but that would change as a result of that sin.. yet God did not change because God does not change.. **Malachi 3:v6**.. That means, sexual intercourse between man and woman in the confides of a sacred holy marriage remains right in the sight of God.. **Hebrews 13:v4**.. In following this way, it will be evident that the couple have done according to His instruction and will be blessed, for blessing is in the word of the Lord.

pg 239

Read

..[Genesis chapter 3]*..Read all from your* ***OKJB.. [Malachi 3:v6]*** *For I am the Lord, I change not; therefore ye sons of Jacob are not consumed...* ***[Hebrews13:v4]****.. Marriage is honorable in all, and the bed undefiled: but whore mongers and adulterers God will judge.*

Cross-reference

Pausing here for a span, the picture is clear what God did to set in motion His plan for a good creation with the right plane and setting, through the man and woman, though different anatomy's they would fit together the course was set and the faithful creator was right there with them as long as this arrangement was upheld. This arrangement however was not upheld and eventually broken, changing the right and good position to a wrong and bad one, yet God remained true to His person, to who He is, He could not change yet something had to change. No longer could the same close relationship between God, the man and woman (mankind) be sustained what followed would be a future where the offspring generations of Adam and Eve would be caught up in a consequential life of choice through choice, now that there was another possibility or path to follow or go along (the evil way) opened up, yet God the creator remains for ever and for all time periods the same, As time progressed mankind would delve further the things opposed to God, and what will happen after breaking the commandments ignoring the warnings of God which has had everlasting painful consequences for mankind as a whole, effecting the coming offspring and generations with all kinds of diseases and sickness bringing sorrows and death despite the warnings.. **Genesis 19** The word of God does not allow for compromise or excuses, men having sex together, women having sex together is not something created by God, it can produce no good fruit, those who sanction such behavior to be good and right considering it to be on the same level as the original will suffer

Cross-reference

the wrath of God. **Romans 1:v18-32**.. because it cant be.

Read

[Romans 1:v18-32]..For the wrath of God is revealed from heaven against all ungodliness and unrighteousness of men, who hold the truth in unrighteousness Read from your **original King James bible OKJB.[Romans:1 verses 18 to 32]**..

REALITY *of* ***REALITY***

MOVEMENT NUMBER 28

Bearing Witness

Bearing witness to the great deeds of God is not unreal. It's a REALITY.

Cross-reference

BEARING WITNESS

To live and at the end of it, try to pretend to God that He did not exist, will be futile, there are so many witnesses, Jesus Christ of course came through the ages to stand in his Fathers stead, Jesus would be all that God is in a man, flesh and blood like any other person, he went on to calm storms, give life to the dead, sight to the blind, feed the hungry, resist all the temptations of the evil one, forgive sinners, walk on water, Jesus loved in word and deed, paying for the sins of the world with his sinless body and blood, his life on the cross at calvary, not putting up a fight or any resistance.. **John 19:v18**..his own people that he came to redeem crucified him, yet he could say.. forgive them Father for they know not what they do.

Read *[John 19:v18]..Where they crucified him, and two other with him, on either side one, and Jesus in the midst.*

The sign of the cross stands for all as witness to the presence of God, every soul and person ever concept-ed from the beginning of mankind until its end, that God the Almighty is a loving forgiving heavenly Father, willing that no one should perish but live with him forever in his kingdom of peace.. **John 3:v16**..

Read *For God so loved the world, that he gave his only begotten son, that whosoever believes in him should not perish, but have everlasting life..**[John 3:v16]**..*

Cross-reference

In my referring to the presence of the Lord God I include the entire creation, the universe, the physical earth, the spiritual heavenly places, to the depths of the earth which gives reference to hell, the prophet Jonah was three days and nights in the belly of the fish for his disobedience, he surely was very scared.. **Mathew 12:v40** certainly knowing the reason why, and so it is in the places of the living dead imprisoned for their disobedience..**1 Peter 3:v1.**

pg 198

pp 114 /1

Read

*..[**Matthew 12:v40**].. For as Jonas was three days and three nights in the whales belly; so shall the son of man be three days and three nights in the heart of the earth..[**1 Peter 3:v19**].. By which also he went and preached unto the spirits in prison.*

Witness to His very existence and activities in making Himself known are some great deeds over nature remembered and told by ordinary people. **Psalm 77:11-15**..here the psalmist writes his praises in remembering God's miraculous commanding of nature when the Lord fought for His people's release held captive and used as slaves for over 300 years at the hand of the Egyptian leaders to build their pyramids and temples.. **Exodus 9-12 and Exodus 12:v31/32** His word (spirit) and these pyramids and temples (earth) stand today bearing witness of the greatness of God, His word will not return to Him void yet will accomplish the thing that He pleases.. **Isaiah 55:v11**.. Creating physical actions in a few spoken words that will be remembered and spoken of for as long as the earth remains.

Cross-reference

Read

*[**Psalm 77:11-15**]..I will remember the works of the Lord: surely I will remember thy works of old. I will meditate also of all thy work, and talk of thy doings. Thy way, O God, is in the sanctuary: who is so great a God as our God? Thou art the God that doest wonders: thou has declared thy strength among the people. Thou hast with thine arm redeemed thy people, the sons of Jacob and Joseph. Selah.*
*[**Exodus 12:v31/32**]..And he called for Moses and Aaron by night, and said, Rise up, and get you forth from among my people, both ye and the children of Israel; and go, serve the Lord, as ye have said. Also take your flocks and your herds, as ye have said, and be gone; and bless me also..[**Isaiah 55:v11**].. So shall my word be that goeth forth out of my mouth: it shall not return to me void, but it shall accomplish that which I please, and it shall prosper in the thing whereto I sent it.*

pg 37

pg 48 Read

*Read all [**Exodus chapters 9-12**] in your original king James bible.. **OKJB.***

The story continues to the red sea where another great miraculous act of Gods omnipotence over nature takes place, first though His spoken word through His servant Moses as the now released Israelites had found themselves facing an un passable red sea, the Egyptians had given chase and were close behind them vowing to slay everyone, at the command of God, Moses tells the frightened Hebrews to be silent and see the salvation of the Lord.. **Exodus 14:v13**..Moses lifts up his hand with the staff held up commands the sea to divide making a way where there was no way and so the people of God could go through on dry land escaping the Egyptian armies. What followed sealed

Cross-reference

the fate of the Egyptians, their horses and chariots, as they pursued the Israelites entering the now dry passage through the red sea in the hope of catching up with them, the Lord told Moses again to stretch out his hand over the red sea and the waters came back over the Egyptians over their chariots, over their horseman destroying them all.. **Exodus 14:v27-28**.. Again both word and the action bear witness to the presence of the Lord and His love devotion to His own those whom hear and accept His voice.

Read

*[**Exodus 14:v13**].. And Moses said unto the people, Fear ye not, stand still, and see the salvation of the Lord, which he will shew to you to day: for the Egyptians whom ye have seen to day, ye shall see them again no more for ever..[**Exodus 14:v27-28**].. And Moses stretched forth his hand over the sea, and the sea returned to his strength when the morning appeared; and the Egyptians fled against it;and the Lord overthrew the Egyptians in the midst of the sea. and the waters returned and covered the chariots, and the horsemen, and all the host of Pharaoh that came into the sea after them; there remained not so much as one of them.*

Bearing witness of the love and truth of God and His willingness to save, not to be miss interpreted, God does not need or have reason to show off His power. God did not build the great pyramids, yet his people the Israelites because they turned their ways from him, giving way to other God's, as a punishment he took his restrictive hands away from them allowing the Egyptian armies to overpower them taking them captive enslaving them for more than 300 years,

Cross-reference

it was during this period that the pyramids and the temples of the Egyptian kings were built using the blood sweat and tears of the Israelites, until God heard their cry for freedom.. **Psalm 137:v1**.. and worked his miracles as mentioned in a show of willingness to come to the rescue, those whom cry out to him with all their heart in complete trust.. **Proverbs 3:v5**..The pyramids stand to this day as a visible witness to these great deeds of God.

Read

*[**Psalm 137:v1**]..By the rivers of Babylon, there we sat down, yea, we wept, when we remembered Zion.. read all of **Psalm 137** in your original king James bible. [**Proverbs 3:v5**]..Trust in the Lord with all thine heart: and lean not unto thine own understanding.*

pg 206

pg 89

The Lord's willingness to make his salvation a witness has led Him to put a plan in to action involving some very specific weaponry to defeat the evil one and his followers..[**1 John 5:v8**].. And there are three that bear witness in the earth, the Spirit, and the water, and the blood: and these three agree as one. Spirit is the Holy spirit..[**John 14:v26**].. Water is baptism.. [**Matthew 3:v11**]. Blood is Jesus life, death on the cross for the sins of the world His resurrection. [**1 Peter 3:v18**].. having been called and accepted these three components out of the salvation plan of God, the spirit itself beareth witness with our spirit that we are the children of God: and if children, then heirs; heirs of God, and joint-heirs with Christ; if so be that we suffer with him, that we may be also glorified together.. [**Romans 8:v16-17**]..

pp 111 /58

pg 246

pg 269

REALITY *of* ***REALITY***

MOVEMENT NUMBER 29

Feelings and Emotions

No feelings and emotions, No Jesus and God.

Cross-reference

FEELINGS AND EMOTIONS

Two gifts not to be taken for granted nor ignored, these gifts have been passed to humankind as part of the person the creator, these very feelings and emotions are what goes on inside the Lord for the same reasons, when these are stirred in a person, man or women, boy or girl the same is stirred within Him, He has to endure the same,

until those Feelings and Emotions no longer exist within the person, the

RR ***Reality of Reality*** when this is allowed to happen, God is no longer present in the person, but the devil, one no longer feels anything, no happiness or sorrow, just an empty shell of blankness for oneself, for others, no sense of care, darkness is all around and inside that person, there is no light even the glint in the eye has gone, all because these qualities have been ignored over and over again, over time, a real pity to allow oneself to drop so low in life, not even to feel sin and shame, the hurt caused to another,lose: the sense of being human all control of these gifts of emotions and feelings to feel nothing not even love for God, neighbor and oneself.. ***Matthew 22:v37-40***.. to a point of no return.

pp 144 /269 /279 Read *..**[Matthew 22:v37-40]**..Jesus said unto him, Thou shalt love the Lord thy God with all thy heart, and with all thy soul, and with all thy mind. This is the first and great commandment. And the second is like unto it, Thou shalt love thy neighbor as thyself. On these two commandment hang all the law and the prophets.*

When the creator created His creation, the first man Adam and then out from Adam the first woman Eve, God in his

Cross-reference

words words were now fulfilled, having said.. let us make man in our own image and after our likeness.. **Genesis 1:v26.. a**nd he felt good at what he had done.. **v31.**
God the creator is referring to all of himself, triune, three persons agreeing as one (God) Father Son (Jesus) spirit (holy spirit/ghost) and at this time the triune God gave to the man dominion to freely take good care of His creation, to rule over it, with the same feelings and emotions, in other words, do a good work, for it was created out of love and with joy for all of it, for His pleasure and when one of the three feel sad all three feel sad and so on.. **Genesis 6:v6.**.
Feelings and emotions are real, when we humans shed tears and weep because of pain and sorrow, especially when our loved ones have to die.. so to does God's .. **John 11:v35**.. it is good to make mention that He only has thoughts of peace and not of evil.. **Jeremiah 29:v11-13** toward us humans.. God can also get quite angry.. **John 2:v15-16..**
His feelings and emotions suffer with ours. And so we come to the point, when something doesn't get used or taken care of in this natural life, for instance, put aside and forgotten, a motor car left unattended, stuck in a garage, the paintwork fades, rust and decay set in, the engine will not run, the interior loses its appeal, when the cutter is not kept oiled and sharpened, over time things become in effectual, the same happens with our feelings our emotions, decayed over time by sin and shame.

Read

..[Genesis 1:v26]..*And God said, let us make man in our imagine, after our likeness: and let them have dominion over the fish of the sea, and over the foul of the air and over the cattle, and over all the earth, and every creeping thing, that creeps upon the earth*

Cross-reference | Read | ***..[Genesis 6:v6]..*** *And it repented the Lord that he had made man on the earth, and it grieved Him at His heart..****[John 11:v35]..*** *Jesus wept..* ***[John 2:v14-16]****..Read from your* ***OKJB.***

pg 70 | Read | ***..[Jeremiah 29:v11-13]..*** *For I know the thoughts that I think toward you, says the Lord, thoughts of peace, and not of evil to give you an expected end.*
Then shall you call upon me, and you shall go and pray unto me, and I will hearken unto you.
And you shall seek me, and find me, when you shall search for me with all your heart.

Ignoring and constantly ignoring our own feelings our own emotions and losing control will lead to all kinds of sins and offenses committed against heaven and earth, life will have no direction and meaningless, nothing good or right can come out of such an emotionless heartless state of being wandering aimlessly. God being the source out of which feelings and emotions come is able to control them, however for this to happen, one must engage His love and truth out of His word and Gospel of Jesus Christ,it will be through this word of God either change of attitude/ behavior evoking these gifts will be kept active and alive and in the right position, plainly said in our heart, the seat of all our feelings and emotions, our very person and being, the non material self, when God dwells in our heart we will retain this.. lets create man in our imagine and after our own likeness certainly a lifestyle without these two qualities is a lifestyle without God and everything that goes with it and nothing good or right will come,

Cross-reference

a vagabond life that is chosen and lived.. **Genesis 4 v12..** nothing good or right will come from it.

Read ***..[Genesis 4:v12]..*** *When thou tills the ground it shall not henceforth yield unto thee her strength: a fugitive and a vagabond shalt thou be in the earth.*

By realizing this is actually happening and wanting to reverse the condition will lead one back into a close proximity with God, he will not refuse nor ignore anyone, no matter how far its gone, when the desire is there, to repent and change, when one reaches a turning point that means that these two gifts have not totally been lost through a choice to throw them away, things in life have just become heavy and burdensome.. **Matthew 11:v28-30.** Calling on the name of the Lord in times of trouble will cause him to come to the rescue, there is help to restore lost or muddled up feelings and emotions, Jesus is here, and willing to restore these lost gifts to their fullness, Jesus Christ knows only too well how and why people need to keep them in good use, he used them whilst visiting the earthly realm, keeping in close proximity to his heavenly Father throughout his own time in the difficulties of a life in the flesh brings, feelings and emotions are a God-Send as the saying goes. Having no emotions and no feelings is like being spiritually dead, not caring about anyone or anything, feeling nothing for yourself or the next person, God can not be in such a lifeless condition, because He is alive and He cares about everyone, about all life styles, in each persons well being, He sent Jesus for the good of mankind both here in this life and the next. These gifts keep us striving on through the hardships of life, Joy, calmness, patience, hope working together will keep alive our confidence that there is a better future with Christ soon to come and

pg 23

Cross-reference

a better position and place for all holding onto these two God given gifts.

Read *..**[Matthew 11:v28-30]**.. Come unto me, all you that labor and are heavy laden, and I will give you rest. Take my yoke upon you, and learn of me; for I am meek and lowly in heart: and ye shall find rest unto your souls. For my yoke is easy, and my burden is light...**[Luke24:v30-33]**.. And it came to pass, as he sat at meat with them he took bread, and blessed it, and broke it and gave it to them. And their eyes were opened, and they knew him; and he vanished out of their sight, and they said one to another, Did not our heart burn within us, while he talked with us by the way and while he opened to us the scriptures?..*

pg 165

pg 249

pg 273

Read The entire chapters from your **OKJB.** To be with Jesus Christ is to have feelings and emotions.

Some bible verses to consider in no particular order..

Read **Psalm139:v14**(happy)**Philippians4:v6** (anxious) **Isaiah12:v2**(fear) **Isaiah 49:v13**(joy) **Matthew 6:v34**(anticipation) **Matthew 11:v28** (tired) **Joshua1:v9** (courage) **John 16:v33** (confident).

Joshua 1:v9 (courage) and Isaiah 49:v13 (joy) These two gifts work together for the good (of God) that something is right and good or the opposite, wrong and bad, at an outbreak persons are invited to examine within themselves, which one of the two categories these feelings and emotions fall into, what has brought them on, what has caused them, by studying right Holy scripture and with heart rendered believing prayer, suppressed or lost feelings, emotions will be restored, re kindled leading back to that missing close proximity with God.

REALITY *of* ***REALITY***

MOVEMENT NUMBER 30

The Judge

God will judge everyone according to their works or no works.

Cross-reference

THEJUDGE

In this I refer not just to any Judge, neither am I referring to a judge appointed by earthly governments, I am also not alluding to magistrates appointed by the same capacity and measures. I am talking about the Almighty God and Judge of all judges **Psalm 75:v7**.. He whom judges this physical world, with the same measure will judge the spiritual worlds, Jesus words I quote : in my Father's house are many mansions.. **John 14:v2**.. Meaning many different conditions some of these conditions are extreme to say the least, just as some live in their earthly mansion to the extreme, the Royalty, rich and famous. Mansions in this regard mean a dwelling place by act or condition.

Read *__[Psalm 75:v7]__..But God is the judge: he puts down one and sets up another. In my Father's house are many mansions: if it were not so, I would have told you I will go to prepare a place for you..__[John 14:v2]__*

pg 198

God the Judge is the creator of all that which is to be judged, that includes all other judges, courts Jury's and magistrates, anyone in fact that proclaims a right or wrong verdict to an action or non action upon another person if not in the right position to do so or in no position.. **Matthew 7:v1-5**.. To be in the right position one must follow the words as spoken by the apostle Matthew, first remove the beam, the blockage in ones eye or life by acknowledging that sin and overcoming it through grace, which is all of the divine influence upon the heart and

Cross-reference

learning from it, and then one can cast out the mote out of thy brothers eye, this God will not judge.

Read *[**Matthew 7:v1-5**]..Judge not, that you be not judged. For with what judgment you judge, you shall be judged: and with what measure you mete, it shall be measured to you again. And why behold thou the mote that is in thy brother's eye, but consider not the beam that is in thine own eye? Or how will thou say to thy brother, let me pull out the mote out of thine own eye; and behold, a beam is in thine own eye? Thou hypocrite, first cast out the beam out of thine own eye: and then shalt thou see clearly to cast out the mote out of thy brother's eye.*

God will judge that which has been judged and the judger or jury, meaning that the judgment of a man is not necessarily the final Judgment, meaning also that in the event of wrong judgment being carried out either by mistake, through conspiracy or other, God will have his final say.. **Romans 2:v1-6**.. no man can get away with anything that has not been rendered as righteous by the ***ALMIGHTY*.**

Read *[**Romans 2:v1-6**].. Therefore you are inexcusable, O man, whosoever thou art that judge: for wherein thou judge another, thou condemn thyself; for thou that judges doest the same things. But we are sure that the judgment of God is according to truth against them which commit such things. And thinks thou this, O man, that judges them which do such things, and doest the same, that thou shalt escape, the judgment of God? Or despise thou the riches of his goodness and forbearance and*

Cross-reference

Read *long suffering; not knowing that the goodness of God leads to repentance? But after thy hardness and impenitent heart treasures up unto thyself wrath against the day of wrath and revelation of the righteous judgment of God; Who will render to every man according to his deeds.*

There are two possibilities to judging both of which are based on fact or truth which is evidence, without which no right judgment can take place, it is not possible for God to make a wrong judgment, and He cannot be judged by any other.

RR The ***Reality of Reality*** is that with whatever judgment a person judges another the same judgment will be measured back, certainly this is not condemning righteous judgment or judging yet a strict code of measurement is to be applied which is truth with love, because God will judge both the judged and the judges, surely there is such a thing as righteous judgment.. **John 7:v24**.. this righteous judgment will be deemed so done in this regard, that regard will always come back to the saving of the soul or leading the soul to Jesus to be saved, for Jesus did not come to judge the world but save.. **John 12:v47**..

Read ***[John 7:v24]**.. Judge not according to the appearance, but judge righteous judgment..* ***[John 12:v47]**.And if any man hear my words, and believe not, I judge him not: for I came not to judge the world, but to save the world.*

This sheds a brighter light on the positions of judges appointed by governments for these

Cross-reference

judges and or magistrates are to realize that they will come under the very same judgment that they mete out, irrespective whether they are making judgments relating to mans laws that have nothing to do with God or His ten commandments, it is worth mentioning that there is no Governing authority on this earth that has not been authorized by the Almighty God, for He is the creator and designer of all power and authorities and governments.. **Romans 13**..

pp 143/ 226/ 271

Read *[**Romans 13:v1**]..Let every soul be subject unto the higher powers. For there is no power but of God: the powers that are ordained of God.*

Certainly judging without having the appropriate evidence or an eye witness goes against all that God teaches in Jesus Christ for Jesus is also the advocate with the Father a propitiation (atonement) for all sins..**1 John 2:v1-2**.. For God the Father is the beginning and end of all things, going by this one said this and that one said that, is not righteous judging, not having all the facts and evidence or wrong motives can be very damaging to souls to the point that they feel betrayed and helpless taking sides or standing up for a person or group because of partiality will draw to a painful outcome based on a wrong judgment that will have to be undone, and will be by the one righteous Judge and his advocate.

Read *[**1 John 2:v1-2**]..My little children, these things write I unto you, that ye sin not. And if any man sin, we have an advocate with the Father, Jesus Christ the righteous And he is the propitiation for our sins: and not for ours only, but also for the sins of the whole world.*

Cross-reference

Partiality and favoritism will also come under the spotlight of righteous judgment because its widespread, a common evil practiced amongst those in high leadership positions, showing respect is a well worn out reason, an excuse for so doing, yet God says; that he is no respecter of persons.. **Acts 10:v34** Meaning that He judges everyone with the same measurement according to him set in the same word, for there is no other to be mete out a measurement, and he alone for none other that knows every person better than they know themselves. **Romans 12:v6** taking all these into righteous consideration when making any judgment not wanting to condemn, but save through Jesus Christ.. **John 3:v17**..

pp 210 /276

pg 122

Read

[Acts 10:v34]..*Then Peter opened his mouth and said, Of a truth I perceive that God is no respecter of persons..**[Romans 12:v6]**..Having then gifts differing according to the grace that is given to us, whether Prophecy, let us prophecy according to the proportion of faith..**[John 3:v17]**..For God sent not his son into the world not to condemn the world: but that the world through him might be saved.*

pp 194 /267/13

Standing back or walking away, watching another speak or do unrighteousness, and not saying or doing anything, is not righteous according to the first Gospel of the apostle John the apostle of love and truth..

Read

.1 John chapter 3..*in your original king James bible **OKJB** and put the words into action.*

REALITY *of* ***REALITY***

MOVEMENT NUMBER 31

Numbers 1 and 2

Let your Yes be Yes: and your No be No.

Cross-reference

NUMBERS 1 AND 2

Life as we know it cannot exist without numbers, that means we need to be aware of them and how they work to benefit us, they can also work against us,

RR

Reality of Reality is based on these two numbers 1 and 2, they are inseparable.

RR

linked in movement, ***Reality of Reality*** are movements from one condition or state to another, from taking an apple to actually eating it, taking steps one and two, movement from darkness to light, from light to heavy, out of man (Adam)came woman (Eve).. **Genesis 2:v23**..For right movement to take place, **1** and **2** must come together or join as spoken, its easy to say I will go to the shop for you that's part **1**, but not go that's part **2** no right movement happens, in this scenario numbers **1** and **2** have not joined so they cannot work for us, therefor work against us, saying yes or agreeing to do something yet not doing so means no right movement, the yes word to do something must be followed through with another yes that it has been done to cause right movement.. **Matthew 5:v37**..Saying no to something works the same way, when saying NO after much deliberation realizing its wrong or just doesn't feel right, the NO must remain for right movement.

pg 189

Read

[Genesis 2:v23]..*And Adam said, This is now bone of my bones, and flesh of my flesh: she shall be called woman, because she was taken out of man. But let your Communication be: Yea, yea, Nay, nay.. for whatsoever is more than these comes of evil.*

Cross-reference

Communicating No or refusing to do or agree must be followed with the same action, that way there is no evil, a change of heart can come later. Christ can change and use people that are decisive..

..Acts 9:v1-8..However God cannot use anyone that is not decisive, whose heart is this way then that way blowing like the wind or lukewarm.. **Revelation 3:v16**..

Read

pg 34

pp 70/71

*[**Acts 9:v1-8**]..And Saul yet breathing out threatenings and slaughter against the disciples of the Lord, went unto the high priest. And desired of him letters to Damascus to the synagogues, that if he found any of this way, whether they were men or women, he might bring them bound unto Jerusalem. And as he journeyed he came near Damascus: and suddenly there shined round about him a light from heaven: And he fell to the earth, and heard a voice saying unto him, Saul, Saul, why persecutes thou me? And he said, Who art thou Lord? And the Lord said, I am Jesus whom thou persecutes: it is hard for thee to kick against the pricks. And he trembling and astonished said, Lord, what wilt thou have me to do? And the Lord said unto him, Arise and go into the city, and it shall be told thee what thou must do. And the men which journeyed with him stood speechless, hearing a voice, but seeing no man. And Saul arose from the earth; and when his eyes were opened, he saw no man: but they led him by the hand, and brought him in to Damascus.[**Revelation 3:v16**]. So then because you are lukewarm, and neither cold nor hot, I will spew you out of My mouth.*

Cross-reference

Lets take a look at nature at how these numbers **1** and **2** show themselves as **fixtures**, some examples: man and woman, light and dark, heavy weight, light weight, difficult and easy, high mountain low mountain, tall and short, its as easy and simple as writing it, these two must come together in some way or another these are evidence of the significance of these two digits, lets have a look at some bible examples and references: Jesus Christ appeared in the physical creation during the compilation of the new testament, yet these are His words about His appearance too in the old testament; Think not that I am come to destroy the law or the prophets: I am not come to destroy, but to fulfill. **Matthew 5:v17**.. these words of Christ link the first testament to the second testament that they agree as one, lets go to another example, Jesus son of man bible verse.. **Luke 24 :v7** and son of God bible verse.. **Matthew 14:v33**..And so in these become true right examples when **2** follows **1** by the right action, these are right movements the spoken word and same action, what Jesus said would happen, happened.

Read

pp 14
3 /130
/100 /29

*..**[Matthew 5:v17]**.. Think not that I am come to destroy the law, or the prophets: I am not come to destroy but to fulfill.. (**1; law, 2; prophets,**).. **[Luke 24:v7]**.. Saying the son of man must be delivered into the hands of sinful men, and be crucified and the third day rise again.. **[Matthew 14:v33]**. Then they that were come into the ship came and worshiped him, saying, Of a truth thou art the Son of God.*

Cross-reference

Two parts: Number 1 and number 2 coming together either to reveal someone or something fits or doesn't, is right or wrong, can be trusted or can't, how is it with us, are we saying one thing and doing another or not doing what we have said? Is our Yes; Yes, our No; No? Only in this way will we move righteously forward, making a false acknowledgment knowingly will lead to No right or forward movement and certainly No gain or profit: lets look at some examples from the Holy Bible; I will choose two… Saul of the Old Testament was anointed king to righteously rule over the people

Read of God.. **1 Samuel 9:v27-10:v1**.. Saul had to give his consent before the anointing, that he would obey the voice of God and he did at first, but did not keep to it and wandered away from his commission ending up suffering, not

pg 98 only did Saul lose His Kingdom the

Read holy spirit left him too.. **1 Samuel 16:14**.. Thc other example I will take from the new testament : this example emphasizes the seriousness of not following through with the right action.. Two people from holy scriptures new testament fail to keep to their promise to the servant of the Lord, after having agreed, sold some of their possessions were expected to hand over all the proceeds to the servant of

Read God kept part back, this led to their immediate punishment (death).. **Acts 5:v1-10**.. What we say (1) and what we do (2) must match as one, if we say or agree too in words (1) and don't carry out the words with the same action

RR (2) the **Reality of Reality** the consequence will apply the same, either: for the good or bad.

NOTES

REALITY *of* ***REALITY***

MOVEMENT NUMBER 32

The Season of Christmas

Only by celebrating Christmas in the right season
will bring true lasting Joy and Peace.

Cross-reference

THE SEASON OF CHRISTMAS

The worshiping and honoring of the fictitious figure Santa Clause, so called father Christmas and the giving of expensive gifts and presents in this name all the pomp and ceremonies, merry making getting hyped up, has to be one of, if not the biggest lie, deception, the worst governance, most wrongfully taught, lived out celebrations by and amongst humanity since the early years of king idolatry, the making and building non living statue type false Gods, in defiance of the one true living God, continuing to do so even after the Lord delivered his people from Egypt in captivity and slavery.. **Exodus 20:v1-3**..The continuing to build statues of false Gods to worship, refusing to obey and worship the Almighty Lord God even after the many warnings and pleadings to return to him through his God fearing prophets and servants, written and told has to stop NOW !! **Isaiah 2:v17-18**.. **Zechariah 1:v3**..

Read

[Exodus20:v1-3]..

And God spoke these words, saying, I am the Lord thy God, which have brought thee out of the land of Egypt, out of the house of bondage. Thou shalt have no other Gods before Me.

[Isaiah2:v17-18]..

And the loftiness of man shall be bowed down, and the haughtiness of men shall be made low: and the Lord alone shall be exalted in that day. And the idols shall utterly be abolished..

[Zechariah1:v3]..

Therefore say thou unto them, thus says the Lord of Host's; turn ye unto me, saith the Lord of host's, and I will turn unto you, saith the Lord of host's.

Cross-reference

This celebrating of Christmas by many sectors of the human race according to worldly understanding year in and year out, the preparations and build up will be so done out of folly, if Jesus Christ is not the reason and focus with the right and truthful teaching as to who and why Jesus Christ was born on this day its significance and impact for the entire human race in time to come.

To say this is an abomination to the Almighty creator having sent His son to die a gift for mankind is not to be scoffed at, and before it is too late those sectors above should choose to go

RR back to the***Reality of Reality*** the real meaning of this day and teach it again, going back to the sabbath Sunday Christian church praise and worship.

The truth is this: it was God that came to mankind in Jesus Christ, whom will come again bringing both freedom and judgment, Jesus is real and he is alive, at his coming all the people of the earth having participated in this kind of foolishness will realize their folly and errors. God promised to send someone to defeat evil, several thousand years ago, He alone is able to fulfill all that he says he will do, by Godly purpose, this kind of

pg 291 celebrating is nowhere near that specific purpose and reason to celebrate the birth of the savior of the world Jesus Christ and the Christmas day.

The real season of Christmas: God came to earth incarnate in Jesus Christ; meaning God in spirit .. **John4:v24**.. took on flesh and blood so that he could go on to die on the cross for the sins of mankind, and defeat the devil, conquered the power of death and the grave ultimately; in the same selfless deed, to bring peace and good will to all men, glad tidings of great Joy

Cross-reference

and peace everlasting, these are the true gifts coming out of Jesus Christ birth, expensive items and artifacts, manufactured specially for the merry making and partying that often lead to disappointment even conflict are not what this special day is about.. **Luke 2:v10-14**..

Read pg 53

***[John 4:v24]**..God is a spirit: and they that worship him must worship him in spirit and in truth..**[Luke 2:v10-14]**..And the angel said unto them, fear not: for, behold I bring you good tidings of great joy, which shall be to all people. For unto you is born this day in the city of David a Saviour, which is Christ the Lord. And suddenly there was with the angel a multitude of the heavenly host praising God and saying Glory to God in the highest, and on earth peace, good will toward men.*

The real season starts and ends in church, by not joining in the fellowship [spiritual] with other members discussing the kingdom of God, the fullness of who we are worshiping will be missed, holy spirit teachings will be absent.. **Matthew 16 :v18..**therefore the real gifts of peace, goodwill to all men as recorded in scripture will not be present, the ***Reality of Reality*** of the whole Christmas message is over shadowed by the flesh. RR

pp 182 /175 /132 /36 Read

[Matthew 16:v18]**.. And I say also unto thee, That thou art Peter, and upon this rock I will build my church; and the gates of hell shall not prevail against it.. **[1 Corinthians 12:v2-27]**.. Read all verses from your **OKJB

Because of the serpent, disobedience, evil and wickedness entered man, so God promised that he would intervene.. **Genesis 3:v14/15**.. Not to force man to obey him but to give an alternative

Cross-reference

to following the evil one, yet God will oppose and destroy all that which does not come from him, as he did in the time of Noah, when evil and wickedness of man increased.. **Genesis 6:v5**.. These events are not to be ignored or taken as a once off, God will act again to destroy all kinds of evils and all wickedness, status and earthly wealth He will not respect.

Getting back to the real story and the

RR ***Reality of Reality*** of the Christmas event. Governments have failed to promote it, but haven't failed to promote commercialism, raking in huge monetary income from the sale of goods, manufactured and sold, even on the Sabbath seventh day in the name of Christmas, covering up the essence;

The Almighty God entering the human sphere in His son Jesus Christ WOW !! what really could be better to promote, the king of kings, Lord of Lords, the creator, the heavenly Father walking with and among the poorest of the poor, sitting down with the sinners, a not for worldly profit event. Its worth making mention of, spreading such good news to your people, your nation, subjects.. instead disobedience the ignoring God's commandments and wickedness prevails.

Read *And the Lord God said unto the serpent, Because thou hast done this, thou art cursed above all cattle, and above every beast of the field; upon thy belly shalt thou go, and dust shalt thou eat all the days of thy life: And I will put, enmity between thee and the woman, and between thy seed and her seed; it shall bruise thy head, and thou shalt bruise his heel..*

Cross-reference

Read .. ***[Genesis 3:v14-15]***.. *And God saw that the wickedness of man was great in the earth and saw that every imagination of the thought of his heart was only evil continually.*

The real focus of Jesus Christ and the Christmas story, brought by and kept burning: through religious instruction classes in schools, the dedicated loving Grand parents who would pass on their faith knowledge, the many Christian church buildings holding regular divine services utilizing the Sabbath day of rest as is its purpose, now not the focus has brought with it ignorance of the truth, yet should not become or considered an acceptable excuse for this ignorance.
The promoting and the sale of goods as if in celebration of the birth of Jesus Christ the son of the living God, in replacement for the right teaching of the gospel of Jesus and the good news of Christmas, will lead to an empty celebrating, the presents and gifts, things asked for and given that will be discarded or eventually just perish, as will the gesture, yet what God offers will be everlasting, through his only begotten son Jesus Christ, who paid for our transgressions with his life that mankind can live things that will never perish mentioned above and the freedom from all guilt and shame. **Isaiah 53:v5**..

Read ***[Isaiah 53:v5]***.. *But he (**Jesus**) was wounded for our transgressions, he was bruised for our iniquities: the chastisement of our peace was upon him; and with his stripes we are healed.*

Cross-reference

And so any other teaching about Christmas, in the using of mythical non real characters, vain celebrations and feasts will yield nothing but calamity against the participants, this is the

RR **Reality of Reality,** the wrong side, certainly it will be pleasing to the Lord and His heavenly host's for the celebrating to go ahead in the right season of Christmas, in the right manna, the right season of Christmas is of expectation, referred or known by true Christians as Advent.

Jesus Christ came into this world of man as is described above and will come again [advent] this thought and belief of an event such as this happening again, to knowing and understanding and accepting its real significance as is told in the four synoptic [linked] Gospels, kept alive by true right worship, together in celebrating the healing and comforting of miracles and wonders the revealed mysteries of the kingdom of God truths taught right and prophecies of old and new fulfilled, so much that .. I just cannot imagine anyone knowing just some of this if not all would choose to trade being part of this great event, to be part of this amazing eternal story, this gift of all gifts for something else, something that temporal, judicable that can never match or compare to this.

pp 27/ 28/ 260

Read *.**[Exodus 20:v7]**.Thou shalt not take the name of the Lord thy God in vain; for the Lord will not hold him guiltless that taketh his name in vain.*

NOTES

MOVEMENT NUMBER 33

Man's Laws

Man's laws will be judged by God's commandments.

Cross-reference

MANS LAWS

Man's laws are not God's laws, the real difference being: man's laws force and punish making people, families, societies financially and spiritually poorer often putting the ordinary into stress and hating the righteous laws of God, these laws of man do not cater for unforeseen circumstances, nor the desire and willingness to comply, yet the opposite, which is where right important to Christians.. **Acts 5 :v27-29..**

However !! even Christians are called to obey the governments.. Romans :v13 whom themselves are called to obey Him.. for there is no higher power than the Almighty by which other powers are ordained, all powers are from God.

And so at the end of everything, all governments and high authorities and powers that break the laws of God, that means just even one of His ten commandment and teach others to do so, could come under His full judgment.. Matthew 18:v6. Governments and higher authorities, rulers and leaders, parents and teachers, churches and institutions, will

pg 227

be judged stricter because of this. **..James 3:v1..** Repentance action is to be made very swiftly should this message be fitting to some.

Read

*[**Acts 5:v27-29**]..And when they had brought them, they set them before the council: and the high priest asked them, saying, Did not we strictly command you that you should not teach in this name? and, behold, ye have filled Jerusalem with your doctrine, and intend to bring this man's blood upon us.. Then Peter*

pp 143 /209 /271

*and the other apostles answered and said, We ought to obey God rather than men. .[**Romans 13:v1-2**].. Let every soul be subject unto the higher powers. For there is no power but of God: the powers that*

Cross-reference

Read

*be are ordained of God. Whosoever therefore resists the ordinance of God: and they that resist shall receive to themselves damnation..**[Matthew 18:v6]** ..But whoso shall offend one of these little ones which believe in me, it were better for him that a millstone were hanged around his neck, and the he were drowned in the depth of the sea. **[James 3:v1]**..MY brethren, be not many masters, knowing that we shall receive the greater condemnation.*

pg 226

God does not need money, however governments do and has to come from the people of the land, this in itself is not wrong, Jesus said when he took a penny and asked? Whose is the image and superscription on it.. **Mark 12:v17**..having said this: by the implementing and enforcement of laws, governments and powers have coveted both the rich and the poor, and by doing so have transgressed the laws of God, where it commands not to covet.. **Romans 7:v7**.. It is just not good enough to keep adding more and more laws, because with each law comes a set of conditions and punishments, trying to live a life pleasing God and pleasing governments brings about a clashing, that clashing is whom is being served, God or mammon?..**Matthew 6:v24**..no person whether Government or slave is free of God's laws and commands, yet these same laws and commands make free, when they are kept not out of fear and terror but out of a love not willing to dissappoint. **Exodus 20:v6**.. Mammon references money and owners of it.

pp 28/ 223/ 260

Read

*..**[Mark 12:v17]**..And Jesus answering said unto them, render to Caesar the things that are*

Cross-reference

Read

Caesar's, and to God the things that are God's. And they marveled at him Read before and after ***[v17]****..in your original king James bible.* ***[Romans 7:v7]****..What shall we say then? Is the law? God forbid. Nay, I had not known sin, but by the law: for I had not known lust except the law had said, Thou shalt not covet..* ***[Matthew 6:v24]****..No man can serve two masters: for either he will hate the one, and love the other: or despise the other, Ye cannot serve God and mammon..****[Exodus 20:v6]****.. And shewing mercy unto thousands of them that love me, and keep my commandments.*

pp 293 /241 /181 /77

pp 27/ 223/ 260

Simple man induced laws are not in themselves wrong or outward inflicting, like some safety regulatory ones, traffic laws and rules for driving cars on open roads, general safety in and around work and public places, right use of certain tooling machinery and equipments to name some would certainly have been incepted for those right purposes. These kind in a sense give an introduction to the benefit of well thought out life saving laws and simple easy to follow rules, they also don't contradict any of Gods own, its rather as if God is saying to those in the high places, I entrust, I actually give you dominion over the proper use of technologies and inventions in the best interest of My creation's natural resources and future wellbeing of all mankind, yet this part has been purposely overlooked by the worlds rich nations, overlooked because of the hunger for natural wealth, power and the desire to protect that wealth, yet at the expense and detriment to this beautiful environment, planet and the

Cross-reference

ultimate survival of mankind. God does expect his ten commandments and laws, ordinances and statutes to be incorporated into all the governing authorities own law systems, these should be like a growing root of all governance, teaching institutions, rulers, leaderships parents, Royalties all are to be properly observed both in word and deed, there shall be consequences for not doing.. **Deuteronomy 11**..thus the Lord has spoken.

Read

*[**Deuteronomy11**]..Take heed to yourselves, that your heart be not deceived and ye turn aside, and serve other Gods, and worship them. And then the Lord's wrath will be kindled against you, and he shut the heaven, that there be no rain and that the land yield not her fruit; and lest ye perish quickly from off the good of the land, which the Lord giveth you. Therefore shall ye lay up these words in your heart and in your soul, and bind them for a sign upon your hand, that they may be front lets between your eyes, And ye shall teach them your children speaking of them, when thou sit in thine house, and when you walk by the way, when you lie down, and when thou rises up. And thou shalt write them upon the door posts of thine house, and upon thy gates.*
*Read all of chapter 11. from your **OKJB.***

It is not to be ignored that God is not selfish and not a God with any wrong motives or intentions towards us or what He has created, through choice that's His choice He has created mankind to be free choosing beings with absolutely no restrictions on what a person does with that choice, however those in the high places in

Cross-reference

positions that by their choice affects others adversely will not go unnoticed, certainly if any affects his own. The folly of focusing squarely on mans laws, just to remain a good law abiding citizen, forgetting or not even considering God's laws and ordinances, to live a life of staying out of trouble with local authorities would be real folly, to accept a job or career offer whereby special or priority treatment will be received or to get a higher position certain conditions will be met is also foolish, to be partial or accept partiality treatment is commonly practiced in society, as if it's the norm however, though a worldly practice, it is better to resist and follow the ordinances of God.. **Colossians 2:v20**.. And be dead with Christ than alive with the world.

Read

.. [Colossians 2:v20] *..Wherefore if you be dead with Christ from the rudiments or elements of the world, why, as though living in the world, are ye subject to ordinances.*

REALITY *of* ***REALITY***

MOVEMENT NUMBER 34

Partiality

A life with God, is a life without partiality.

Cross-reference

PARTIALITY

One terrible human quality that drives unsuspecting people away from the path of righteousness is partiality, a bit like respecter but easier to identify and just as easy to notice in a person, especially if on the receiving end of what it can do. When a person treats people differently because of status or how they dress or look, the position they hold or don't hold or because what they can get out of them, this is showing partiality or being partial, it is wrong, a serious offense in the sight of God a sin against heaven and earth that needs to be forgiven and rectified in other words, through a remorse repentant changed attitude, taking into consideration persons could have been hurt and left scarred even to have been left in less fortunate position in society, their immediate surroundings. It is clear that this partiality attitude and behavior will not yield or lead to any long term benefit to both or all participants, long term meaning beyond this life after the grave. Of course always I take my motivation from and out of the Gospels and life of the Lord Jesus Christ for He showed no partiality, certainly no man could He gain anything from, His total life was given to serving mankind.

For all to have in an abundance, to have life of His life no need of anything more, in

RR *Reality of Reality* He offered and gave the exact same to all persons born that lived past, present and future.. **Hebrews 13:v8**..

Read *..**[Hebrews 13:v8]**.. Jesus Christ the same yesterday, and today, and forever.*

Cross-reference

Nature is the right and good example of impartiality with God the creator of heaven and earth, the Almighty one that just says the word to nature itself the elements sun and rain and they respond accordingly and when they do these natural elements do not single out the evil to rain drop upon only neither the good just to receive the sun rays only, yet both receive what is given and provided out of His righteousness.. **Matthew 5:v45**..

Read *[**Matthew 5:v45**]..That ye may be the children of your Father which is in heaven:for he makes his sun to rise on the evil and on the good, and sends rain on the just and on the unjust.*

pg 285

The Holy scriptures refer to impartiality as the Royal law, to those showing this particular behavior and attitude..
Read.. **James chapter 2 ..** on partiality: **v4**..on the Royal law. This title is not just a symbolic one it's a real one indeed, it alludes to no other than the Almighty God the creator through Jesus Christ, the Lord of lords, the King of kings.. **Revelation 17:v14**.. through Jesus Christ this Royalty is made possible, not the kind of royalty one finds on the earth, quite the opposite, human royalty does not manage to depict the same royalty as the royal law depicts, one that would show no impartiality with its subjects, human royalty rule over their land and people with a partiality type rule, final judgment will be without partiality, earth's royals will be judged not by their royal status and lavish lifestyle, these mean nothing to the Almighty God who is himself a King, coming to earth incarnate in Jesus Christ, giving up his own

Cross-reference

kingdom life to do so all for the sake of the soul of mankind, accepting to be born in a manger, he will judge the heart. To give up the life of partiality living would in all probability lead to giving up a life of luxury high profile living, possibly involve leaving family being cut of from their fortunes and inheritances.. **Matthew 19:v29**.. yet if the motivation is in following a life with Jesus Christ, the reward will truly be the Royal one to

pg 235

last.. **Revelation 5:v10**.. for those who show no partiality to God and their neighbor whilst living on the earth fulfilling the royal law, either through the excepting of the simple poor lifestyle they find themselves in or in the giving up of another lifestyle that restricts them from the impartial living as is expected in fulfilling the royal law, through choice by choice.

pg 123

Read

*[**James 2:v1-9**]..My brethren, have not the faith of our Lord Jesus Christ, the Lord of glory, with respect of persons. For if there come unto your assembly a man with a gold ring, in goodly apparel, and there come in also a poor man in vile raiment and ye have respect to him that wears the gay clothing, and say unto him, sit thou here in a good place; and say to the poor, Stand thou there, or sit here under my footstool: Are ye not then partial in yourselves, and are become judges of evil thoughts? Hearken, my beloved brethren, Hath not God chosen the poor of this world rich in faith, and heirs of the kingdom which he hath promised to them that love him? But ye have despised the poor. Do not rich men oppress you, and draw you before the judgment seats? Do not they blaspheme that*

Cross-reference

Read *worthy name by which ye are called? If ye fulfill the royal law according to the scripture, Thou shall love thy neighbor as thyself, ye do well. But if ye have respect to persons, ye commit sin, and are convinced of the law as transgressors.*

Read ***[Matthew 19:v29]***..*And every one that hath forsaken houses, or brethren, or sisters, or father, or mother, or wife, or children, or lands, for my name's sake shall receive an hundredfold and shall inherit everlasting life.* ***[Revelation 5:v10]****. And hast made us unto our God kings and priests: and we shall reign on the earth.*

pg 233

To experience partiality as one who shows none, not to retaliate is a noble act of faith and a pure quality in itself, that the Lord can accept as righteousness, because He does not.. **Romans 2:v11**..

pp 32/152

Read ***[Romans 2:v11]***.. *For there is NO respect of persons with God.*

NOTES

MOVEMENT NUMBER 35

Money

Man cannot serve God and mammon.

Cross-reference

MONEY

The bible says the root of all evil is the love of money, it continues in the same verse saying that some coveted after it and lost their way.. **1 Timothy 6:v10**..Money in itself is not an evil commodity if sought after and used correctly for the right reasons will benefit many a person even nations, having some most certainly reduces the risk of doing other things, eases the stress caused through living in this natural world.

Read

*For the love of money is the root of all evil:which while some coveted after, they have erred from the faith, and pierced themselves through with many sorrows...**[1 Timothy 6:v10]**..*

pp 120/163

So wide spread is the workings of money and involving it in life that there are so many dangers associated with it, the temptation to do anything to gain it has to be controlled, it is the most coveted possession that a person, family, group or organization can own, once tasting its power, what one can do by having it, will become the driving force behind many deeds and actions, most of which money will be the motive and focus, where it comes from or out of, how it has been obtained often reveals a devious not to be trusted character or ruler, the number one danger and trap is that it becomes a god, hence the word mammon often used to describe it as desire of the flesh, when this happens the victim cant get enough focus on obtaining more and more and making it puts blinkers on to anything else, that something else has more value than all the money in the world.. Jesus offer of salvation, through him

Cross-reference

eternal fellowship with God, a place and state of being that money has no part in, to get there the wealthy just might have to choose to sell what they have and give to the poor.. **Mathew 19:v16-21]..**

pg 290

Read *..[**Mathew 19:v21-23]**..Jesus said unto him, if you will be perfect, go and sell that you have, and give to the poor, and you shall have treasure in heaven.*
But when the young man heard that saying, he went away sorrowful: for he had great possessions.

When reading more and understanding into Jesus teaching in this story, the young man was not an unruly person, or evil person he observed the commands and laws of God, yet could not do this one thing.

pg 29

What Jesus is showing in this parable, is that to follow him, nothing must be too hard to do or give up, time does not stand still with it can come many changes in character by temptations certainly to obey the law just because its a law is not necessarily a gesture of love, yet to give of one's goods or possessions freely to a neighbor IS, to belong to Jesus assembly it could be that there are the needy among the assembly, further to share goods is to share in the will of God to provide for all, building Godly character. Read

pg 190

Read verses.. **Mathew 19: 16-20** in your **OKJB.**

Read *.. [**Malachi 3:v8-12]**..Will man rob God: Yet ye have robbed me. But ye say, Where in have we robbed thee? In tithes and offerings. Ye are cursed with a curse: for ye have robbed me, even this whole nation. Bring ye all the tithes into the store house, that there may be meat in mine house, and prove me now here with,*

Cross-reference

Read

says the Lord of Hosts, if I will not open the windows of heaven, and pour you out a blessing, that there shall not be room enough to receive it.
And I will rebuke the devourer for your sakes, and hes hall not destroy the fruits of your ground; neither shall your vine cast her fruit before the time in the field, says the the Lord of hosts.
And all nations shall call you blessed: for you shall be a delight-some land, says the Lord of hosts.

Money, natural wealth in itself cannot absolutely influence where souls end up after dying, neither does having lots of money in the bank or no money influence or impress the Lord, yet the Lord can look favorably upon the poor in spirit persons not seeking after (earthly desires).
The poor in spirit are persons whom consider natural wealth, money and fame not a priority in life, to be poorer in the natural spirit is to be wealthy in the heavenly spirit..
Mathew5:v3 certainly to remain in a good and right position with the Almighty God is to seek first the kingdom of God, and build up for yourself treasures in heaven.
Having lots of money and the status that goes with it, will not influence life span, for when the soul of a person is required of God that is it, whether any preparation work has been done in this regard or none, this could then be too

RR

late. The ***Reality of Reality*** is that a person can not serve God and mammon which is money ..
Mathew :6v24.. Jesus Christ completes the astonishment by stating why? for he will hate the one and love the other or else, he will hold to the one and despise the other.. this is the danger with money it can become the secret master over a person, when God should be the master.

Cross-reference

striving for monetary wealth can lead and invariably does into a totally dark position in life, some very serious crimes against heaven and earth has been money driven leaving the culprit wrecked spiritually, one such historical figure was Judas Iscariot of biblical history fame, he sold out Jesus Christ to the chief priests and elders for 30 pieces of silver.. **Matthew 27:v3/5**.. though he tried to repent by returning the coins, the deed had been done, setting in motion the non changeable consequences that would follow.

Read *[**Matthew 5 :v3**]..Blessed is the poor in spirit for theirs is the kingdom of heaven. [**Matthew 27:v3/5**]..Then Judas, which had betrayed him, when he saw that he was condemned, repented himself, brought again the thirty pieces of silver to the chief priests and elders. Saying, I have sinned in that I have betrayed the innocent blood, and they said, what is that to us? See thou to that. And he cast down the pieces of silver in the temple, and departed, and went and hanged himself..*

pp 293 /228 /181 /77

Read *[**Matthew 6:v24**]..Read this chapter from your **OKJB**.*

Money should be acquired naturally, not supernaturally, this means a fair price paid for a fair deed done or a right cost charged in exchange for the right thing purchased, it should never be that one uses their advantage or upper hand to extract more than is needed to realize huge profit, of course it's a big world, the playing field is open yet the onus is on both the buyer and seller to even the field of business, by keeping the trade off fair and right where greed is kept out of the exchanging money transaction, that it boils down to need and need, not want and want.. **Micah 6:v10-12**..

Cross-reference

Read *[**Micah 6:v10-12**]..Are there yet the treasures of the wickedness in the house of the wicked, and the scant measure that is abominable? Shall I count them pure with the wicked balances, and with the bag of deceitful weights? For the rich men thereof are full of violence, and the inhabitants thereof have spoken lies, and their tongue is deceitful in their mouth.*

The Holy Bible warns all of mankind the dangers that come with earthly wealth of spent energy sunk into achieving fame and fortune, no matter how much money a person has in the bank, it can not be used to buy everything, no amount of money can buy God's favor.. **Acts 8:v19-20**.. nor can it be exchanged for a single sin committed, or get into the kingdom of God.. **Mark 10:v25**.. Still God can use a man's wealth to bring him to humility and honor.. **Proverbs 18:v11/12**..

Read *[**Acts 8:v19-20**].. Saying, Give me also this power, that on whomsoever I lay hands, he may*
pg 183
*receive the Holy Ghost. But Peter said unto him, Thy money perish with thee, because thou hast thought that the gift of God may be purchased with money.. [**Mark 10:v25**]..It is easier for a camel to go through the eye of a needle, than for*
pg 293
a rich man to enter the kingdom of God..

Read *[**Proverbs 18:v11/12**].The rich man's wealth is his strong city, and as an high wall in his own conceit. Before destruction the heart of man is haughty, and before honor is humility.*

REALITY *of* ***REALITY***

MOVEMENT NUMBER 36

Kingdom of Heaven vs Kingdom of God

The kingdoms of God are not eating and drinking, YET within.

Cross-reference

KINGDOM OF HEAVEN VS THE KINGDOM OF GOD.

Yes God is the King of King's, this creation belongs to Him, He is the owner, what happens to heaven and earth at the end of the day God decides, and so it will not be surprising to hear these words.. God is King of everything, all other kings must bow to Him, in any life any sphere.. **Revelation 19:v16**..

The kingdom of heaven first. The reason first or before the kingdom of God is just that, one up from the earth sphere, one before the kingdom of God, it's the the place of the living dead, yes the spirit world, it has no physical dimensions unlike the earth, there is no time to determine how long one has been there or how long one will remain there, when one considers the advantages of time only, this position or condition where there is no time for those whom did not take advantage of the gift of time whilst in the flesh on earth, will find that they are disadvantaged, simply because time is a gift, its grace, there would have been grace opportunities time related should these opportunities was not recognized and not taken advantage of.. **Romans 13:v11.. Luke 12:v20..**

pg 104

Read

*[**Revelation 19:v16**]..And he hath on his vesture and on his thigh a name written **KING OF KINGS, AND LORD OF LORDS.** [**Romans 13:v11**]..And that, knowing the time, that now it is high time to awake out of sleep: For now is our salvation nearer than we believed. [**Luke 12:v20**]..But God said unto him, thou fool, this night thy soul shall be required of thee: then whose shall those things be, which thou hast provided?*

pp 155/ 280/ 294

Cross-reference

Entering the kingdom of heaven unprepared is as good as throwing away ones natural life, in other words wasting it, in this last few words, I am not referring to those who passed on out of un-natural or forced circumstance before the full life term had been reached, these such souls God will judge accordingly, He will even the paths righteously, my concern for writing this is for those still able to read these writings and act on them. The kingdom of heaven is either a realm of peace and rest for those who had prepared themselves by accepting the grace offered during the earth life choosing to follow the Lord Jesus Christ orientated themselves OR a place of unrest and disorientation for those who did not.. **Luke 16:v19-31**.. just were not prepared, it will be the way it was; the measures that were taken before arriving in the kingdom, the measures that would have been made available through revealing opportunities called Grace that were rejected by choice now become past or spent Grace opportunities. All is not lost though ; there is still some comfort to know, the message and truth brought here in this chapter of this ***Reality of Reality*** book, is that God is still the Sovereign King, his unfathomable love and mercy still abound there. However this will be somewhat different in that some had already chosen their fate, and now find themselves disorientated or lost, perhaps captive in their iniquities not able to move around and come and go as it was with them in the earthly realm, the result of a first life lived rejecting or not knowing Jesus Christ whom frees. NOW !!

pp 25/ 26/ 76/ 169/ 278

RR

Cross-reference

pg 100

these souls of the deceased rely on help and intervention to come from outside of their bondage, either by way of prayer, supplication and pleading with Jesus Christ to be merciful.. Acts 12:v5.. Or through visiting, by Jesus himself or him sending his true servants..1 Peter 3:v19..

Even through Jesus true believing members of the body of his church, in any of these gracious means; family, friends even enemies to the not known can be helped, anyone wanting to be.

pg 169

Read [***Luke 16:v19-31***]..*Read all verses from your original king James bible.* ***OKJB.***

Read [***Acts 12:v5***]..*Peter therefore was kept in prison: but prayer was made without ceasing of the church unto God for him. And when Herod would have brought him forth, the same night Peter was sleeping between two soldiers, bound with two chains: and the keepers before the door kept the prison. And behold the angel of the Lord came upon him, and a light shined in the prison: and he smote Peter on the side, and raised him up saying, arise up quickly. And his chains fell off from his hands. And the angel said unto him, Gird thyself, and bind on thy sandals. And so he did. And he saith unto him, Cast thy garment about thee, and follow me. And he went out, and followed him; and wist not that it was true which was done by the angel: but thought he saw a vision. When they were past the first and the second ward, they came unto the iron gate that leadeth unto the city; which opened to them of his own accord: and they went out, and passed on through one street; and forthwith the angel departed from him...*[***1 Peter 3:v19***].. *By which he also went and preached unto the spirits in prison.*

Cross-reference

PRISON is used to describe a condition of bondage, this can happen in the flesh and spirit or both at the same time, tied or bound to a place or condition.

When a soul and spirit enters the next life finding itself in a prison type state because of wrong behavior towards Christ and neighbors, the only way of change is through Jesus Christ and those he wronged, the tables are now reversed, quite a turn around of the roles and position, thats the
RR **Reality of Reality** of the situation.

The very one rejecting love and truth in the first life, now realizes that is what it needs, this event is not to be confused with the event described in our bible verse with Peter and the angel, for Peter was put into prison for following his Lord, it was Jesus who sent the angel to free Peter, answering to the faithful prayers of the church of Christ.

Jesus has the God given power to free the bound the imprisoned, he can free from any kind of bondage, in this life and the next. Entering the heavenly realm, [place of the dead] with Jesus is total freedom and peace, freedom from the bounds that sins brings, those finding this peace, (a feature of the heavenly kingdom) would have sought Christ by selling their goods and giving of some earthly desires to follow him and obtain it, before entering there.

Matthew 13:v44.. So how did these souls obtain this feature, it says in v45 that they looked for it, diligently, they wanted it, selling things to purchase this peace, certainly not gold, nor silver or money, but worldly characteristics like: pride, arrogance, power hungry, self righteousness, greed, disobedience, a life filled with sin and shame, loveless life style.. all of these have the same denominator, these chosen conditions would course spiritual blindness, blinding souls from seeing the true and real treasures of the kingdom of heaven

Cross-reference

to be found on the earth though are not treasures easily come by among the world"s greater populations, yet without such treasures it will surely be impossible to have peace and rest in the kingdom of heaven. ..
(not final resting place).

pp 8 / 290

Read

[Matthew 13 :v44-48]*..Again, the kingdom of heaven is like unto treasure hid in a field; the which when a man had found, he hid, and for joy thereof goes and sells all that he has, and buys that field. Again, the kingdom of heaven is like unto a merchant man, seeking Godly pearls: Who when he had found one pearl of great price, went and sold all that he had, and bought it, Again, the kingdom of heaven is like unto a net, that was cast into the sea, and gathered of every kind: Which, when it was full, they drew to shore, and sat down, and gathered the good into the vessels, but cast the bad away.*

Its worth making mentioning: it says that IN... **[1 Corinthians 13:v4-9].**. It Describes some love characteristics..
Charity suffers long, and is kind; charity envies not; charity vaunts not itself; is not puffed up, does not behave itself unseemly; seeks not her own; is not easily provoked; thinks no evil; rejoices not in iniquity, but rejoices in the truth; bears

Read

all things, believes all things, hopes all things, endures all things; Charity never fails: but whether there be prophecies, they shall fail; whether there be tongues, they shall cease; whether there be knowledge, it shall vanish away, for we know in part, and we prophesy in part.

Cross-reference

The kingdom of God is the next or one up from the kingdom of heaven, yet not the final place of dwelling, its where the throne of God is, its not a physical place but a condition within.. **Luke 17:v20-21**.. it is not meat and drink; but righteousness and Peace and joy in the Holy Ghost.. **Romans 14:v17**..Jesus preached the Kingdom of God on earth, he taught that the kingdom of God is not the world of flesh and blood but opposite, to experience the impact of God in his kingdom on earth and in ones life, the world of flesh and blood must be overcome by seeking first the kingdom of God.. **Matthew 6:v33**..again a matter of choice, choice belongs to faith in Jesus Christ that through him whatsoever is born of God overcomes the world.. ***THE SAINTS.*** **1 John 5:v4/5**..

Read

*[**Luke 17:v20-21**].. And when he was demanded of the pharisees, when the kingdom of God should come, he answered them and said, The kingdom of God cometh not with observation: Neither shall they say, Lo here! Or, lo there! For, behold the kingdom of God is within you..[**Matthew 6:v33**]..But seek ye first the Kingdom of God, and his righteousness; and all these things shall be added unto you.. [**1 John 5:v4-5**]..For whatsoever is born of God overcomes the world, and this is the victory that overcomes the world, even our faith. Who is he that over- cometh the world, but he that believes that Jesus is the son of God?*

pg 204

THE KINGDOM OF GOD IS WITHIN

The kingdom of God is the condition or the state of the soul and spirit of a person brought about through the overcoming power of the

Cross-reference

Holy Ghost, the sacrifice and merit of Jesus Christ and the cross, those who are the called and chosen are the first fruits of men to be redeemed from the earth.. **Revelation 14:v3/4**.. think of a fruit tree, the ripe fruit on the tree are harvested first before they get rotten and fall off or eaten, thereafter the other fruits are harvested when they too are ripe.,time does not stand still. The first fruits (overcomer's) will be harvested first at the return of Jesus Christ and removed from among men, and whisked off to the kingdom of God for the marriage feast in heaven..**Matthew22:v4**.. **Revelation 19:v7-9**.. Life and death will continue as we know it for 42 months or 3 1/2 years while the marriage supper in heaven (spirit world) is celebrated.

pg 114

Read *[**Revelation 14:v3/4**]..And they sung as it were a new song before the throne, and before the four beasts, and the elders: and no man could learn that song, but the hundred and forty and four thousand, which were redeemed from the earth. These are they which were not defiled with women; for they are virgins. These are they which follow the lamb wheresoever he goes. These were redeemed from among men, being the first fruits unto God and the Lamb..* ***The Lamb is Jesus Christ***

Read *..[**Mathew 22:v4**]..Again he sent forth other servants, saying,Tell them which are bidden, Behold I have prepared my dinner: my oxen and my fat-lings are killed, and all things are ready: Come unto the marriage..*
*[**Revelation 19:v7-9**]..Let us be glad and rejoice, and give honor to him: for the marriage of the lamb is come, and his wife has made herself ready.*

Cross-reference

Read

And to her was granted that she should be arrayed in fine linen, clean and white: for the fine linen is the righteousness of saints. And he said unto me. Write Blessed are they which are called unto the marriage supper of the Lamb. And he saith unto me, These are the true sayings of God.

THE KINGDOM OF HEAVEN IS NOT THE FINAL PLACE.
But one up from the earthly.

NOTES

REALITY *of* ***REALITY***

MOVEMENT NUMBER 37

Statues and Monuments

Statues and monuments are dead visible things. God is alive yet invisible.

Cross-reference

STATUES AND MONUMENTS

Made from anything and everything under the sun, in any shape or form, with a head, eyes, limbs a body, made out of gold, precious gem stones, bronze, clay or stone, wood from the tree; it makes no difference to the likeness of a person or the greatness of a structure the value, they cannot talk, or walk, think and make decisions, move, they have no life in them, they are dead things, no matter how much time or how many people it takes to carve one or build one, the price tag paid they will never have a soul or a spirit, it cannot grow up and get old, bear children solve mysteries of: the universe, the Kingdom of heaven,the spirit world the past nor present or the future, they have no life, they are "lifeless" and the Almighty God hates them, He abhors mankind that He created and gave life of His life too, in His image and after His likeness, replacing Him with lifeless idols. ..**Exodus 20:v4/5**.. **Psalm 115:v4-8**..

pg 117

Read ..***[Exodus 20:v4-5]..****Thou shalt not make unto thee any graven / molten image, or likeness of anything in heaven above or in the earth beneath, or that is in the water under the earth. Thou shall not bow down thyself to them, nor serve them for I the Lord thy God am a jealous God, visiting the iniquity of the fathers upon the children unto the third and fourth generation of them that hate me.*

Read ..***[Psalm 115:v4-8]..****Their Idols are silver and Gold, the work of men's hands. They have mouths, but they speak not: eyes they, but they see not: They have ears but they hear not:*

Cross-reference

Read

noses have they, but they smell not. They have hands, but they handle not: feet they have, but they walk not: neither speak they through their throat. They that make them are like unto them: so is every one that trust in them.

Yet the people of the earth refuse to resist this temptation time and time again that has severe consequences, not least those wanting to be worshiped and or remembered for something they have done or as if they are something great and powerful themselves, no one other than the Almighty God IS, and that's all there is to it. Governors and world leaders are placed by God in their governing positions to stamp out such acts of lawlessness activities happening amongst the nations, yet they are not doing so. Biblical history has many examples of kings having made larger than life images in defiance of this particular commandment, Neb-u-chad-nezzar was one such king, made a decree throughout his kingdom that at the time ye hear the sound of the music everyone must fall down and worship the golden image that the king hath set up.. **Daniel 3.**. warning that anyone falls not down to worship the golden image would be thrown into the fiery furnace. And so at the set up of this Golden Image, the king did send to gather together the princes, the governors, the captains, the judges, the treasurer's, counselors, the sheriffs, and all the rulers of the provinces, to come to the dedication of the image which Neb-u-chad-nezzar the king had set up..**v2** which they did. However not everyone would be so foolish to disobey their one true living God.. **v12**.. Three Jewish men, Sha'drach, Mes'hach

Cross-reference

and A-bed'-ne-go would not serve the gods of the king, nor worship the golden image, and so were cast into the fiery furnace, yet they believed in their God, that He would deliver them from the burning fiery furnace..**v17**..and so that's what happened the fire did not touch them.. **v25-26..** Unfortunately for the men that threw the three into the fiery furnace were slew by the fire..**v22**..

Read *Read all **[Daniel chapter 3]** in your original king James bible.. **OKJB.***

To erect any kind of statue or monument in remembrance or honor to another human being no matter what has been done or achieved or set in motion, is still an abomination to God, simple because nothing good or right can be achieved without his presence and blessing, for only God is good and righteous.. ..**Mark 10:v18**.. In ***Reality of Reality*** the unseen God is behind and the cause for anything that is worth honoring, his works speak for themselves.

Read *And Jesus said unto him, Why calls thou me good? There is none good but one that is God.. **[Mark 10:v18]..***

The building and erecting of monuments and statues by man is not limited to things that are worthy of honoring, quite often the honoring of that person or group of persons is for atrocities that have no good whatsoever in them, to the point that behind the entire escapade is nothing but sinister motivations, at the great loss and demise of others, this the Almighty God cannot

Cross-reference

be involved with. This is the work of darkness, it grabs hold of unsuspecting high profiled men in high places and positions, drawing others in like a slip stream, blocking out who is the real one with the right power behind anything good and right, that if God were to be called upon through a nature of need and belief in the recognizing that the battle or challenge opposes the goodness and righteousness of God and so this battle or challenge can only be defeated or overcome with His help, and surely freely available. This erecting of statures and monuments in cities, town centers, public places parliamentary buildings etc are most assuredly in the hands of and control of world Governments, yet the people of the land must choose out of their own, to accept and worship by accepting and agreeing to such dead things, remember though whom will be disobeyed. God cannot fight for neither save those whom do not honor and worship Him only, putting Him first is the only way to know God, that's faith in other words.

NOTES

REALITY *of* ***REALITY***

MOVEMENT NUMBER 38

The Sabbath, Seventh Day

The Sabbath day was made for man, not man for the Sabbath, The Seventh day.

Cross-reference

THE SABBATH, SEVENTH DAY

An official rest day for you and for me, on this day one day out of a seven day week, human kind can without doubt or fear take a break from all toiling and tilling for their earth needs, you and I have every right by virtue of the words of the Almighty God and His matching actions.. **Genesis 2:v2**.. Later on in this very same God added His command.. **Exodus 20:v8**.. therefore it comes down to a simple choice, refuse to work for your bosses, even if it means getting the sack.

pp 27/ 28/ 223

RR

The ***Reality of Reality,*** this day is made for man, not man for this day to do as he pleases, so don't become greedy like your bosses, its and answerable offence God will judge both the employer and the employee; even the governments for there part surely they collect in a lot of tax.

pg 162

Read

*..**[Genesis 2:v2]**..And on the seventh day God ended his work which he had made and he rested on the seventh day from all his work which he had made..*
***[Exodus20:v8]**..Remember the Sabbath day to keep it holy.*

God would not make commands that he would not do first, he chose to rest on the seventh day after working to create the world for six days, he leaves all of us with the same choice, why has it been so hard for mankind to choose not too? a simple choice to have a break from hard labor, worship and honor the God of our forefathers, by going into His house on earth, resisting the temptation of the evil one to do something else, have fellowship with other believers and be

Cross-reference

with our families, Jesus did so and spoke about this.. **Mark 2:v25-28**.. It is a law of God not to labor for earthly gain everyday of the week, on the Sabbath the Holy day of the Lord, man is forbidden to work this way, yet other labors can he do, one can work to support someone or something in need.. **Matthew 12:v11-12**..

Read

*..**[Mark 2:v25-28]**..And he said unto them, Have ye never read what David did, when he had a need and was an hungered, he, and they that were with him? How he went into the house of God in the days of A-bi'-thar the high priest, and did eat the show bread, which is not lawful to eat but for the priests, and gave also to them which were with him? And he said unto them, The sabbath was made for man, and not man for the sabbath: Therefore the son of man is also Lord of the sabbath.. **[Matthew 12:v11-12]**..And he said unto them, What man shall there be among you, that shall have one sheep, and if it fall into a pit on the sabbath day we he not lay hold on it, and lift it out? How much then is a man better than a sheep? Wherefore it is lawful to do well on the Sabbath days.*

God will be not overlook the breaking of this law, not even governments or huge companies have the authority nor the power to override the final word of God... **Revelation 22:v14**.. consequences will follow should anyone agree to break this law of God.. **James 2:v10**.. To make things worse, to break one law is to be guilty of breaking all ten..

pg 72

Read

*..**[Revelation 22:v14]**.. Blessed are they that do his commandments, that they may have the*

Cross-reference

Read

right to the tree of life, and may enter into the gates of that city. ***James 2:v10]***..*For whosoever shall keep the whole law, and yet offend in one point, he is guilty of all.*

It is not a hidden fact to any working bread winner of a family who has duties to perform for his employer involving hard labor be it physical or mental that not much else can be done at the same time, and so this day of rest allows the time for other non employed or money earning activities to take place or happen, one such activity this Sabbath day has been designated for is that there will be no excuse for honoring the Lord God, the Almighty creator of Heaven and Earth, even time itself, for He that's God is a jealous God and expects to be honored held in high esteem for He is good.. **Psalm 100:v5**.. Because God is good and all that He does is so good and right, He has made this rest day for all the right reasons, with God there is much right that comes our way, even a day of complete rest, total relaxation, that one can be refreshed as it was with God, this is how he knows what we need before we ask him.. **Matthew 6:v8**..

Read

..[Psalm 100:v5].. *For the Lord is good: his mercy is everlasting: and his truth endures to all generations..*

pp 89 /92 /128

[Matthew 6:v8]..*Be not you therefore like unto them for your Father knows what things you have need of, before ye ask him.*

This is worth making mention of; after Jesus had healed the withered hand of a man outside the Temple on the sabbath day, the group of clever

Cross-reference

people looking on, the Pharisees confronted him, yet Jesus being much wiser than them asked this question.. **Mark 3:v4-6**..sometimes even the truth is alluded by people that refuse to learn from it, yet suffering at the end. Its easy to conj-our up an excuse or reason to open for business on the sabbath day, saying; people have to eat, however because Jesus is Lord of the sabbath too, he will make his judgment, and that judgment cannot be appealed against.. **Matthew 12:v8**..

Read

*..**[Mark 3:v4-6]**..And he said unto them, Is it lawful to do good on the sabbath days or to do evil? To save life, or to kill? But they held their peace. And when he had looked round about on them with anger, being grieved for the hardness of their hearts, he saith unto the man, Stretch forth thine hand, And he stretched it out: and his hand was restored whole as the other. And the Pharisees went forth, and straightaway took counsel with the He-ro'di-ans against him, how they might destroy him.. **[Matthew 12:v8]**..For the son of man is Lord even on the sabbath day.*

Mankind has taken control over using its hours in ways solely for its own benefit in that so much other activity takes place on this day, that really has nothing to do with or about God or Jesus Christ. Governments again fail to uphold this very law of God, by making sure business shopping, entertainment, television are banned or properly governed on this one day, yet there have been time periods where Kings and rulers of nations have, noticeable by the many church and cathedral buildings that stand in and

Cross-reference

around cities, albeit unused and empty, standing as witness to what once was greatly incorporated in governance. And so what should and could be happening around the world and amongst all nations the worshiping of the Almighty Lord God for all His goodness, his Godly providence over the cultural lands, upon mankind as a whole, greater than these still!! are in His tender mercies through His suffering son Jesus Christ, in whom these church and cathedral buildings were originally built, as the heart of every city or village, to remember and keep Holy, just that one day out seven, instead slotted in as if just another day as the other six, no different, yet it is, its HOLY meaning set apart for God's use.. a serious matter not too "make no mistake". Though this day has been widely forgotten by peoples, with God it can never be no matter how it gets pushed out of the way, His own people will keep lifted up this banner of faith.. **Psalm 60:v4.. Isaiah 13:v2**.. He exists in His own people today, nothing and no one can remove, neither ex- extinguish in those that obey this law, for them that do they retain the blessings reserved for them for all time.. **Exodus 31:v16-18**..

Read

*..**[Psalm 60:v4]**..Thou hast given a banner to them that fear thee, that it may be displayed because of the truth..**[Isaiah 13:v2]**.. Lift ye up a banner upon the high mountain, exalt the voice unto them, shake the hand, that they may go into the gates of the nobles..**[Exodus 31:v16-18]**..Wherefore the children of Israel shall keep the sabbath, to observe the sabbath throughout their generations, for a perpetual covenant. It is*

pg 270

Cross-reference

Read

a sign between Me and the children of Israel for ever: for in six days the Lord made heaven and earth, and on the seventh day he rested and was refreshed. And he gave unto Moses, when he had made an end of communing with him upon mount si'nai, two tablets of testimony, tablets of stone, written with the finger of God.

The seventh day or the sabbath day or Sunday as we have come to know it, or the day which the Lord has made, a day of rest, the Holy day, or day of atonement there are more.. all refer to this one Holy day. ***BANNER*** = Standard, sign, belief or faith.

NOTES

REALITY *of* ***REALITY***

MOVEMENT NUMBER 39

The Ten Commandments

Following Jesus Christ is keeping the Ten Commandments.

Cross-reference

THE TEN COMMANDMENTS

Given to the whole world, yet to leaders first (Moses) then to parents and teachers of children and to the future generations, these are the ten commandments and gifts from God to go out into the uttermost parts of the world through teaching. **Deuteronomy 6:v6-9**..to be upheld, not to be forgotten or ignored, these ten commands tell the peoples of the time that God does exist, telling the Israelites(Gods own people) what they should choose to do, choose not do, all that God expects of them to show that they do love their God..**v5**.. to all peoples of that time around the year **1400 BC**.. the worlds population including Gods own had already committed all these abominations, breaking the ten commands before having been given them, had ignored the prophets, the warnings, had distanced themselves from the ways of the Lord, from Him, ignoring history itself, and so the loving God intervened by giving Ten easy to learn commandments in an act to bring His people back into close proximity with him and to know him for who he is.. I am that I am.. **Exodus 3:v14**..I change not..

Read

*..**[Deuteronomy 6:v7-9]**..And these words, which I command thee this day, shall be in thine heart: And thou shalt teach them diligently unto thy children, and shalt talk of them when thou sits in thine house, and when thou lay down, and when thou rise up. And thou shalt bind them for a sign upon thine hand, and they shall be as front-lets between thine eyes. And thou shalt write them upon the posts of thy house,*

Cross-reference

Read

and on thy gates. [v5]..And thou shalt love the Lord thy God with all thine heart, and with all thy soul, and with all thy might.

Summed up as just two commandments by Jesus Christ during his visit to earth which can be read in.. **Matthew 22:v37-40**..these same words spoken by Jesus were exampled by his actions and brought to life the very will and nature of his heavenly Father which in turn is intended to bring all of mankind into the same position and closeness with this same Father, whom wants to be the same loving Father to every soul, for all and eternity to be co heirs with Jesus to His Kingdom **Romans 8:16-18**..

Read

*..**[Matthew 22:v37-40]**..Jesus said unto him, Thou shalt love the Lord thy God, with all thy heart, and with all thy soul, and with all thy mind. This is the first and great commandment. And the second is like unto it, Thou shalt love thy neighbor as thyself. On these two commandments, hang all the law and the prophets...**[Romans8:16-18]**..*

pp 200 /144 /279

The spirit itself bears witness with our spirit, that we are the children of God: And if children, then heirs; heirs of God, and joint-heirs with Christ; if so be that we suffer with him, that we may be also glorified together.

pp 198

Heading back again to before the appearance of Jesus Christ, and the time when God used acts of a physical nature to demonstrate his presence, using ordinary men to carry out his will by instruction, that His great deeds and miracles would add the other side to the stone tablets on which the ten commandments were

Cross-reference

written with his finger.. **Exodus 31:v18**..to give his people a glimpse into this other side of the commandment law giving God, that other side being one that will fight for those choosing to obey them, of course for those choosing not to keep them all to breaking a single one, would mean nothing really had changed the down-ward spiral of moving away from God after having seen the covenant (ten commandments) and the great deeds of deliverances, the evidence is clear that even with all this help and interventions from the loving God not all men will live in peace and harmony.

pg 264 Read

***..[Exodus 31:v18]**.. And he gave unto Moses, when he had made an end of communing with him upon mount Si'nai. Two tablets of stone, written with the finger of God.*

These ten commandments are not introduced to force or to punish, to refuse to obey the commands is why the outcome is the way it is, not the law or command but the choice, which is free, and so too is the choice to teach and uphold them by leaders that includes governments, teachers schools, royalty church's pastors and ministers, parents and individuals..
Deuteronomy 11:v17-22.. And so knowing the ten commandments and yet choosing not to live by them or teach them will lead to the same consequence and when that day comes, all the rewards or wages will be matching to the works done or not done, for the good, or not for the good, for all things said and or done:
The Lord offers a blessing or curse...
v27-28.

Cross-reference

Read

*..[**Deuteronomy11:v17-22**]..*
*Read all 6 verses from your **OKJB** [**v27-28**].. A blessing if ye obey the commandments of the Lord your God, which I command you this day. And a curse, if ye will not obey the commandments of the Lord your God, which I command you this day.*

I will use another word instead of commandment, the word is precept, a general rule intended to regulated behavior, this description or statement shines more light onto the motive or intention the Lord has for sharing some of His intimate characteristics out of His nature, as a leader himself passing the same onto men in leadership positions as set up by Him.. **Romans 13:v1**. Such leaderships would include but not limit.. Governors, Rulers, Kings, Queens Princes and princesses etc These would have been entrusted with the task and accepted, the privilege to see to their own nation, the people of the land upholding these ten commands, and God would definitely provided all the required resources, as he always has done, because He has given these gifts for our benefit, these commandments form part of is grace part of is evidence that will be used at the last judgment **Revelation20:v11-15**.. this tells us that obeying or not obeying these Ten Commands will be recorded both in heaven **and earth.**

pp 143 /209

pg 158

Read

*..[**Romans 13:v1**]..Let every soul be subject unto the higher powers. For there is no power but of God: the powers that be are ordained of God. [**Revelation 20:v11-15**]..And I saw a great white throne, and him that sat on it, from whose face the earth and the heaven fled away; and*

Cross-reference

Read

there was found no place for them. And I saw the dead, small and great, stand before God; and the books were opened: which is the book of life: and the dead were judged out of those things which were written in the books, according to their works. And the sea gave up the dead which were in it; and death and hell delivered up the dead which were in them: and they were judged every man according to their works. And death and hell were cast into the lake of fire, this is the second death. And whosoever was not found written in the book of life was cast into the lake of fire.

These books that were opened are records of a persons life, those that did not obey the commandments did not accept and follow Christ as is recorded in the books and so together with the books(souls)were cast into the lake of fire for all and eternity, those that did accept and followed Jesus Christ have obeyed Gods commandments and so will not suffer the same fate, their names (souls) will be recorded in the book of life to live with God in His kingdom for all and eternity. Governments, Royalty and leaders have the power, authority to project and preserve these ten commandments without force throughout their lands, to watch over and protect their borders ensuring the preservation of these laws, because God Himself will be with authorities and higher powers to fight for them as he has said that he would and done so in the past.. **Deuteronomy 20:v4.. Joshua 1:v2.2 Chronicles 20:v17** certainly a better option than having to answer to that very same God for not so doing.

Cross-reference

Read

pg 204

[Deuteronomy 20:v4]..For the Lord thy God is he that goes with you, to fight for you against your enemies, to save you..**[Joshua 1:v5]**.There shall not any man be able to stand before thee all the days of thy life: as I was with Moses, so I will be with thee: I will not fail thee, nor forsake thee..**[2 Chronicles 20:v17]**..Ye shall not need to fight in this battle: set yourselves, stand ye still, and see the salvation of the Lord with you, O Judah and Jerusalem: fear not, nor be dismayed: tomorrow go out against them: for the Lord will be with you.

God's people (those who keep his laws and commandments). In miraculous ways, God will however act according to His Sovereignty in His or by His word and in his own time, yet be assured says the word, that God will not disappoint.

Whether it be in removing of the enemy (those who keep not his laws/commands) or in providing the protecting power so that his word can be kept alive within the borders of the land, he will provide everything needed and provided there is a genuine faith and trust in His commandment word to physical action.

NOTES

REALITY *of* ***REALITY***

MOVEMENT NUMBER 40

Death

Though all men shall die, with Christ there is NO death.

Cross-reference

DEATH

The separation between man and God is death, this happens when sin is present and not dealt with through the Grace offered by God through Jesus Christ and the message of the cross. There are two deaths, the death of the flesh and blood which is the first death, the second death (always two)of the soul and spirit which is final. God is alive therefore He is life, life comes from Him, when persons go against Him or doubt He even exists doing as they please or whatever pleases them in a manner that excludes the Lord, the
RR ***reality of reality*** is,those who choose a life without Jesus Christ are already condemned to death.. **John 3:v18**.. Yet think themselves to be alive in the things they do, the pleasures in which make them feel satisfied, yet this will be temporary and fade away forever. The physical body will die first and go back to the earth from whence it came, to be dust again for it was formed out of the dust of the earth.. **Genesis 2:v7** never to reform as some may think, or come back reincarnated as something else,these assumptions are far from the truth, this is the first death.. **Genesis 2:v17**.. And so the soul and spirit of a person after having really died the first returns to the spirit world or kingdom of heaven, the life that drove that flesh body lives on albeit.. without the original physical body.

Read ..**[John 3:v18]..** He that believes on him is
pp 194 /210/13 not condemned: but he that believes not is condemned already, because he has not believed in the name of the only begotten son of God.

pg 149 Read *..**[Genesis :v7]..** And the Lord God formed man of*

Cross-reference

Read *the dust of the ground. and breathed into his nostrils the breath of life; and man became a living soul. But of the tree of the knowledge of good and evil, you shall not eat of it: for in the day you eat thereof you shall surely die.*

The second death is the death of the soul and spirit to all that refuse Jesus Christ offer of life, this will be final.. Revelation 20:v14-15.. death and hell will be destroyed, eternal separation from God for all participating, those persons that have ended their life disobeying God will be cast out from His presence forever to which it sought the end will be torment in the everlasting fire along with devil Satan and his angels.. **Matthew 25:v41**.. also referred; the the flame of torment.. **Luke 15v24..**

To be cut off from God is to forfeit all exposure to anything good and right, the place of hell will be the perpetual state of sin, yet those suffering there will be aware of the horrors their sins have brought them, a conscious filled with guilt and shame unending remorse never to be answered, no prospect of release or parole or freedom, justice by righteous judgment has been served.

The choice to reject Jesus Christ love offer is to refuse eternal freedom and get eternal bondage.

Read ***..[Revelation 20:v14-15]..****And death and hell were cast into the lake of fire. This is the second death...****v15** *..And whosoever was not found written in the book of life was cast into the lake of fire.*

..[Mathew 25:v41]..*Then shall he say also unto them on the left hand, Depart from me, you accursed into everlasting fire, prepared for the devil and his angels..****[Luke 16:v24]..****And he cried and said, Father Abraham, have mercy on me, and send Lazarus that he may did the tip of his finger in water to cool my tongue; for I am tormented in this*

Cross-reference

Rejecting to be a child of the kingdom of God will have devastating consequences after experiencing it.. **Matthew 8:v12.**

Read

..***[Matthew 8;v12]***..
But the children of the kingdom shall be cast out into outer darkness: there shall be weeping and gnashing of teeth.

This is the wages or reward of sin.. to reject God, His commands, His presence through Jesus Christ, The holy bible, His servants.. **Luke 16:v25-31**..even signs, there will be no longer the notion that there is goodness in man, to be cut off or separated from God will put an end to that deception once and for all, that all goodness can only come from the Almighty God, and his servants that are here in and throughout the earth actively spreading this good news of life in Christ Jesus. Every day we face the possibility of death, it can come suddenly and unexpected in a car collision or other accident, slowly and painfully through illness, we have no control of that part, yet how we have prepared ourselves for that time we do have a choice too, certainly if we are expecting to die through old age, our lifestyle will bear that right preparation, just by willfully observing two simple laws : love God and thy neighbor as yourself, for on this hangs the law and the prophets..

pp 25/ 26/ 76/ 169/ 245

Read

..***[Luke 16:v25-31]***.. *But Abraham said, Son, remember that thou in thy life time received thy good things, and likewise Lazarus evil things: but now he is comforted, and thou art tormented. And beside all this, between us and you there is a great gulf fixed: so that they which would pass from hence to cannot; neither can*

Cross-reference | Read

they pass to us, that would come from thence. Then he said, I pray thee therefore, Father, that thou would send him to my father's house. For I have five Brethren; that he may testify unto them, lest they also come into this place of torment. Abraham saith unto him, They have Moses and the Prophets; let them hear them. And he said, Nay, father Abraham:but if one went unto them from the dead, they will repent. And he said unto him,if they hear not Moses and the prophets, neither will they be persuaded, though one rose from the dead.

Jesus fulfilled the law and the prophets.. **Matthew 22:v40**..Following him is life, death has no power over following Jesus Christ,because he overcame death with his life

pp 200 /144 /269 Read *..[**Matthew 22:v40**]...On these two Commandments hang all the law and the prophets. Read in your **OKJB** ..Verses **38** and **39.***

Not wanting to know about dying, not wanting to enter into a conversation about dying, worse still not wanting to prepare oneself, for passing from life to death is just as if undertaking a journey, there are things that will go with, things that will remain behind, without proper right preparation for any journey is simply foolish, not to have some knowledge of where one will end up what to expect is
RR unthinkable.. **Luke 12:v20**.. the ***Reality of Reality*** in this movement has come alive in death, live a life in right preparation to die, spending time at funerals is better than at festivals,

Cross-reference

spending time pondering about death is better than spending time having a good time, now this divides the world into two groups of people, the wise in death and the foolish in life. Death is the last enemy of mankind its sting is still having an effect upon those mentioned above, yet not in those who have accepted the one and the only defeater of death, Jesus Christ whom died by crucifixion yet was raised up again to eternal life to be at the right side of His heavenly Father.. **Acts 2 :v31-33**..Oh death where is thy victory, where is thy sting..**1 Corinthians 15:v50-57**..

Read

..***[Luke 12:v20]***.. *But God said unto him, thou fool, this night thy soul shall be required of thee: then whose shall those things be, which thou hast provided?..[Acts 2 :v31-33]..He seeing this before spake of the resurrection of Christ, that his soul was not left in hell, neither his flesh did see corruption. This Jesus hath God raised you, whereof we are all witnesses. Therefore being by the right hand of God exalted, and having received of the Father the promise of the Holy Ghost, he hath shed forth this, which ye now see and hear.* ..***[1 Corinthians 15:v50-57]***.. *Now this I say, brethren, that flesh and blood cannot enter the kingdom of God; neither doth corruption inherit in corruption. Behold I shew you a mystery; We shall not all sleep, but we shall all be changed. In a moment, in the twinkling of an eye, at the last trump:for the trumpet shall sound and the dead shall be raised incorruptible, and we shall be changed. For this corruptible must put on incorruption, and this mortal must put on immortality. So when this corruptible shall have put on incorruption, and this mortal shall have put on immortality, then shall be brought to pass*

Cross-reference

Read *the saying that is written Death is swallowed up in victory. O death, where is thy sting? O grave where is thy victory? . The sting of death is sin; and the strength of sin is the law. But thanks be to God, which giveth us the victory through our Lord Jesus Christ.*

Read *For the wages of sin is death; but the gift of God is eternal life through Jesus Christ our Lord..* ***Romans 6:v23..***

pp 188

NOTES

REALITY *of* ***REALITY***

MOVEMENT NUMBER 41

Governments and Leaders without God

All governance will be over governed by the Lord God.

Cross-reference

GOVERNMENTS AND LEADERS WITH- OUT GOD

God provides all the means to everything for everything, for everyone and everybody under the sun and that's all there is to it, letting the sun shine on the good and bad, the rain to do likewise, Governing or leading with God or without Him completely, is really impossible simply because he is the creator, He has made and provided everything under the sun down to: life the air, time itself yet that's how it appears to be the world round very noticeable with the rich first world governments and dominant world leaders, holding their regular parliaments and summits planning their strategies without so much as a murmur about God the Almighty creator and his commands for good right governance, making any kind of law to bind their own people into submission, these people would not be sat or standing in their positions if it were not come from above, the very chairs that they sit on are made from the trees provided by Him, the wood through can not speak to bear testimony of this, all the other commodities, materials, minerals, fuels and elements just name them, God is the source, He provides the means even the technologies, He is truth and if these things would talk would scream out in praise to this fact.. **John 1:v3**.. and **Colossians 1:v16-18.**.

pp 177/40 Read

*..[**John 1:v3**].. All things were made by him; and without him was not anything made that was made..[**Colossians 1:v16-18**].. For by him were all things created, that are in heaven, and that are in earth, visible and invisible, whether they be thrones or dominions, or principalities or powers: all things were created by him and for him. And he is before all things, and by him and for him.*

Cross-reference

Just as the sun shines on the bad and good and he gives rain to those who do good and those who do evil.. **Matthew 5:v45**..so it is that everyone benefits from the earths resources too, even the poor. A governance of this nature is truly one with no direction, whats more and worse will be one doomed to fail on all accounts with it bringing a variety of eternal consequences first for the leaders and second for the led, there are numerous examples proving evidences in holy scripture to back up these words, that record first how the Lord had governed and still over sees his creation, the fixtures in nature that no local government or power or force NO leader can change,or force on another.. **Genesis 7:v4.. Isaiah 38:v8**..God is the authority over all authorities God does not force how governments and leaders do what they do, he does not force, He has no desire to shut down, on the contrary, he is righteous, there has to be governors and leaderships it is right to have them in place, God will measure these authorities, with the same mcasure as he measures, on the same scales of balances using what the same examples that has all ready been and confirmed in and by the one sent by God; Jesus Christ proclaiming that all authority has been given to him by his Father in heaven on earth.. **John 19:10-11**..

pg 232

Read

*..**[Matthew 5:v45]**..That ye may be the children of your Father which is in heaven: for he makes his sun to rise on the evil and on the good,and sends rain on the just and the on the unjust...**[Genesis 7:v4]**.. For yet seven days,and I will cause it to rain upon the earth forty days and forty nights; and every living substance that I have made will I destroy from off the face of the earth. ..* ***[Isaiah 38:v8]..***

Cross-reference

pg 131

Behold; I will bring the shadow of the degrees down in the sun dial of Ahaz, ten degrees backward, so the sun returned ten degrees, by which degrees it was gone down.

Read

..[John 19;v10-11]..*Then said Pilate unto him speak thou not unto me? Know you not that I have power to crucify thee? and have power to release thee? Jesus answered.*

Thou couldest have no power at all against me , except it were given thee from above: there fore he that delivered me unto thee has the greater sin.

When governance is not God focused, His own that is followers of Jesus Christ the Christians will come under persecution from the governors when faced with the choice to obey God or them in the event that any of the laws of God are swept aside, this is a very serious transgression God considers against Himself.. **Matthew 25:v32**.. yet done unto mere people sometimes perhaps seemingly one of no importance as the bible verse claims, status to significance in terms of world related, influences God nothing. God is no ***respecter of persons,*** the worlds leaders put in authority by Him, no matter how powerful they think they are and no matter how bad or good any world authority assumes, all will be answerable to the one whom has authority over all authorities, the Almighty God and He will have the final say, his word will conclude all is said and done.

Read

*..**[Matthew 25:v32]**..And before him shall be gathered all nations: and he shall separate them one from another, as a shepherd divide his sheep from the goats.*

Cross-reference

God will deal harshly with anyone who offends his own people, meaning wrongfully teaches or suppresses the true nature of God to the point of causing any of the least of God's own to stumble in their belief and trust in Him.. **Mark 9:v42**..the word of God through Jesus Christ must be lived and taught right by leaders, governments that impose their laws and unhealthy high tax burdens by enforcement and punishing will not go unseen by the Almighty God who rules over all nations, whom sees what cannot be seen by men..
..**Psalm 22:v28..** And so ruling and governing not considering and or bringing in the input of God, will result in wrong governance, the miss use of the resources provided by the provider will result in a multitude of sins committed against heaven and earth that will have to be in due season brought out in the open and dealt with by Him.

RR The ***Reality of Reality*** here is clear, those men in high ranking positions are not above the laws and commands of God, they apply equally to all and everyone everywhere and should be taught so.

Read *..**[Mark 9:v42]**..And whosoever shall offend one of these little ones that believe in me, it is better for him that a millstone were hanged around his neck, and he were cast into the sea..**[Psalm 22:v28]**..For the kingdom is the Lord's and he is the governor among the nations.*

I now go to an example from of old, types of governance that God abhors, taken from the old testament out of the life of Daniel, he was renown for being God fearing, a decree was made by the assembled presidents, governors, princes, counselors, captains and signed into law by the King Darius of the time, that if anyone was to ask a petition of any God or man other than the King himself is to be cast into the den lions..

Cross-reference

Daniel 6 .. Of course Daniel would be caught praying to his God as he always freely did giving his enemies cause to have him thrown into the den of lions, however Daniel's God shut up the mouths of the lions and he came out unscratched, as a result, Darius the king having realized that he had been tricked into signing the decree, had Daniel's accusers cast into the den. This is a stern warning to all governors mentioned, not to rule by force, not to cause anyone to stumble..

Read

*Read all of.. **[Daniel 6]**... in your original king James bible. **OKJB.***

GOATS ARE THE STUUBORN, THE HARD HEARTED PEOPLE.

REALITY *of* ***REALITY***

MOVEMENT NUMBER 42

Being Rich in Goods

Worldly treasures can be used to purchase heavenly treasure.

Cross-reference

Having lots of money in itself is not forbidden by the Almighty God, Jesus did however allude to money and earthly possessions holding one back from having something so much more valuable.. **Matthew 19:v21-23**... Monetary wealth and everything that comes with.. huge rambling properties, expensive cars, high end lifestyle is likely to be a draw away from the kingdom of heaven than towards it, this is because the kingdom of heaven is not made with human hands or created by the mind of humans on the contrary at the expense of;better put at the giving up of the physical part. Treasures of the natural kind are for the existence upon the earth, yet people tend to seek after them as if they make them powerful, untouchable, even to consider themselves as blessed, and say: I deserve what I have because I have worked hard, the truth of it is; they are temporal treasures of the earth, and can do nothing to prolong life nor gain the upper hand when it comes to exiting the earth in death over any other. These earthly kind of treasures as mentioned here are not hid, freely available, definitely obtainable, any prospector of earthly store will be able to obtain it, what one actually does to obtain it may not be favorable in terms of dealing righteously and fairly with their neighbors however the real treasure that is hidden and not easily to obtain "the kingdom of heaven", Jesus says what should be done to possess it after finding it.. **Matthew 13:v44**..

pg 239

pp 8 / 248

Read

*..**[Matthew 19:v21-23]**..Jesus said unto him, if thou wilt be perfect, go and sell that thou*

Cross-reference

Read *hast,and give to the poor,and thou shalt have treasure in heaven:and come and follow me.*
*But when the young man heard that saying, he went away sorrowful: for he had great possessions..**[Matthew13:v44]**. Again,the kingdom of heaven is like unto treasure hid in a field; the which when a man hath found he hide, and for joy thereof goes and sells all that he hath, and buys that field.*

In this parable, the field is the world, the treasure hidden the field or world is the kingdom of heaven a good place of peace and readiness while waiting for the Lord to come, to possess the kingdom the mad must give up his worldly treasures in exchange for the kingdom of heaven where God rules. God is not a physical being that can be touched or held,He has no need to gather earthly goods what will He do with things pertaining to this world when He is not of this world ..**John 4:v24** ..he therefore did not create this earthly world to represent Him with natural riches and goods, and so striving for and storing up to amassing any kind of physically sought after riches be them touchable or non touchable, treasures out of the earth gold and silver the elements and minerals to paper awarded qualifications or other recognizable merits presented out of the standards developed for this world, neither impresses nor counts with God for spiritual wellbeing and salvation.

pg 219

Read *..**[John 4:v24]**..God is spirit: and they that worship him must worship him in spirit and in truth.*

Cross-reference

What does impress God [for understanding only] when belongings are shared with neighbors, or those that have share with those that don't, the needy, retaining just enough for themselves and family, not to gather up more than is necessary to survive, over indulgence and greed often is what drives people to be rich in goods for status are unable to perceive that to be prominent and important in this life is not possible without being rich in goods, such persons can not associate being naturally poor with this kind of lifestyle and find it hard to give away or share things of importance to them.

Having a certain amount of natural wealth is not wrong in itself, family inheritance often can't be avoided, what makes being rich in goods harmful to a soul and spirit of a person is what it brings out in that person, and who they become in character, or how the riches or position were obtained, were others hurt along the way, was partiality and favoritism part of the process, was neighbors of the rich person such as employees unfairly treated or paid as little wages as possible, were authorities bribed or friendships made that these low wages and long hours of hard labor to employees also part of the equation to obtain the status of being rich in goods, this part of how, why, what happened to get there can be worse than the actual having of the goods or wealth. The worst that can happen, which is really sad, a complete remoteness to God, meaning a close proximity to the devil now becomes evident, for a tree is known by its fruit.. **Luke 6:v43**.. every thing does work the same, and what might seem to be a blessing in these riches could be the far from that, the devil having complete control of that person, God can longer influence a change in this life.

Cross-reference Read *..**[Luke 6:v43]..** For a good tree brings not forth corrupt fruit neither does a corrupt tree bring forth good fruit.*

Jesus had this to say about striving in life and the choices we have.. **Matthew 6:v24..**

pg 242

pp 241 /228 /181

*..**[Mark 10:v25]**.. It is easier for a camel to go through the eye of a needle, than a rich man to enter the kingdom of God..**[Matthew 6:]**.. **[v24]**..No man can serve two masters: for either he will hate the one, and love the other; or else he will hold to the one, and despise the other, Ye cannot serve God and mammon..**[v31-34]**.. Therefore take no thought, saying, What shall we eat? Or What shall we drink? Or Wherewithal shall we be clothed? (For after these things the Gentiles seek:) for your heavenly Father knows that ye have need of all these things. But seek ye first the kingdom of God, and his righteousness; and all these things shall be added unto you. Take therefore no thought for the morrow: for the morrow shall take thought of the things for itself. Sufficient unto the day is the evil thereof.*

RR The ***reality of reality*** it would be a better treasure to give up or sell earthly type possessions which also often come with worldly attitudes of greed and power to buy or possess put on the kingdom of heaven treasure of peace and contentment and accept what God provides for the morrow, for he said: be anxious for nothing.. **Philippians 4:v6-7** ..than to lose ones soul in attaining worldly store.. Read the bible verses **Luke.. 12:v22-30** ..on how God will take care of His own that trust and obey Him, these are His disciples **(v22)** a disciple of Jesus is he that follows His every word they are separated from a life that seeks and strives for earthly riches as described above, in verses: **16- 21** of this same

pp 89/204

Cross-reference

Luke 12 ..Jesus tells a parable a story about a man storing up treasures filling up barns full of stuff, only to have his soul called that same night leaving all the goods behind for others to divide,

Read

pp 89/204

*..[**Philippians4:v6-7**]..Be careful (anxious) for nothing; but in everything by prayer and supplication with thanksgiving let your requests be made known unto God.*
And the peace of the God, which surpasses all understanding shall keep your hearts and minds through Christ Jesus.

Read

*..[**Luke 12:v16-21**]..And he spake a parable unto them, saying, The ground of a certain rich man brought fourth plentifully:And he thought within himself saying What shall I do, because I have no room where to bestow my fruits ? And he said This will I do: I will pull down my barns, and build greater; and there will I bestow my fruits and my goods. And I will say to my soul, Souls thou hast much goods laid up for many years; take thine ease, eat, drink, and be merry. But God said unto him, Thou fool, this night thy soul shall be required of thee: then whose shall those things be, which thou has provided? So is he that lays up treasures for himself, and is not rich toward God.. Read the other verses from your original king James bible. **OKJB.***

It is worth making mention of: during the exodus from Egypt to the promise land, through Moses God commanded the Israelites during wandering in the wilderness that they were to gather enough manna and quail sufficient for one day, God is teaching His people and people everywhere from all time periods to obey him, God knows what is needed and will always provide enough for those whom obey Him with blessing.

Cross-reference

On the sixth day the Israelites were commanded to gather enough to eat for two days, enough for the sabbath day also in other words, this is in line with the law of the Sabbath that it is a Holy day, a day of resting from all labors, God saw ahead to all time periods that man would use this Holy sabbath day also to gain more than is naturally needed, more than is really sufficient, certainly the earth needs time to replenish itself, people need their rest too.

God is in control, when the Israelites tried to find more on the Sabbath, there was none that was edible.

*..[**Exodus 16:v15-30..**Yet some tried to gather on the sabbath day, but found none..*
Read all 15 verses from ***OKJB.***

AMEN AND AMEN

The end

INDEX

1 Without a life in Christ, there can be no proper rest or peace in this life or the next.

2 Saying one thing and doing another has the same result now and forever.

3 Accept and follow the will of God for it is a fixture that can never die.

4 Our nature either reflects the nature of God or the nature of the devil.

5 Everything returns to the beginning or source whether good or evil.

6 To speak God's love, one must feel the relief out of Jesus' sacrifice of love.

7 Only through unity in Jesus Christ will give us unity in everything else.

8 Right / right equals right outcome. Wrong / wrong equals wrong outcome. Right / wrong equals wrong outcome.

9 Whatever the outcome of our lives, we have free willed it that way.

10 The same life lived on earth will be the same life lived after death in the grave.

11 However God / Jesus Christ the word remains Holy.

12 Prayers are a gift and covenant agreement.

13 It's up to the individual to recognise the Lord's Hosts, He is here.

14 Royal Status in this life does not guarantee the same in the next life, yet could be the opposite.

15 The number three is perfection in God or in the devil.

16 Idolatry in any form is tempory gain with eternal consequences.

17 Favouritism or partiality in any manner will not bring the same with God.

18 God is willing to save from eternal death, yet will not willing to force.

19 Man will not turn off the supply that feeds his own diseases.

20 All high power and governance is subject to the higher power GOD.

21 Our body and life is not just ours.

22 There will always be one more thing to be done, choose, and do.

23 Automation will bring automated sickness and disease.

24 A life with Jesus Christ is total freedom. Without him, total bondage.

25 One original. Many fakes.

26 The church of Christ has no name IT is hidden in the word of God.

27 God does not change, mankind has to choose to.

28 Bearing witness to the great deeds of God is not unreal. It's a reality.

29 No feelings and emotions, no Jesus and God.

30 God will judge everyone according to their works or no works.

31 Let your Yes be Yes: and your No be No.

32 Celebrating Christmas in the right season will bring true lasting Joy.

33 Man's laws will be judged by Gods commandments.

34 A life with God, is a life without partiality.

35 Man cannot serve God and mammon.

36 The kingdoms of God are not eating and drinking, YET are within.

37 Statues and monuments are dead visible things. God is alive yet invisible.

38 The Sabbath was made for man, not man for the Sabbath.

39 Following Jesus Christ is keeping the Ten Commandments.

40 Though all men shall die, with Christ there is no death.

41 All governance will be over governed by the Lord God.

42 Worldly treasures can be used to purchase heavenly treasure.